Using Art in RE Using RE in Art

Vivien Northcote

The National Society
A Christian Voice in Education

a co-publication with
Church House Publishing

The National Society/Church House Publishing,
Church House,
Great Smith Street,
London SW1P 3NZ

ISBN 0 7151 4916 4

Published 1999 by The National Society (Church of England) for Promoting Religious Education and Church House Publishing

Cover design by Leigh Hurlock

Printed by The Cromwell Press Ltd, Trowbridge, Wiltshire

Contents

Acknowledgements

I would like to acknowledge with grateful thanks all the support I have received during the preparation of this project from Hamish Bruce and all the staff at Church House Publishing; from Alan Brown and Alison Seaman of the National Society; and from Jennifer Speake. I would also like to acknowledge the wisdom of all those art historians and scholars whose insights and writings have provided such an inspiration to me. They are far too many to list here, but without their earlier work this book could never have been written. Lastly, I would like to thank my family for all they have done to encourage and support me. This book is for them all.

The author and publisher gratefully acknowledge permission to reproduce copyright material in this book. Every effort has been made to trace and contact copyright holders. If there are any inadvertent omissions we apologize to those concerned and will ensure that a suitable acknowledgement is made at the next reprint.

HarperCollins Publishers Ltd: 'Fynn', *Mister God, This is Anna* (1977, pp. 170 ff.; 1st edn William Collins Sons & Co. Ltd, 1974).

HMSO: Extract from the National Curriculum is Crown Copyright and is reproduced by permission of the Controller of HMSO.

Qualifications and Curriculum Authority: RE Model Syllabuses, SCAA (1994).

Penguin Books Ltd: Extract from the Second Revelation (pp. 76 ff.) in Julian of Norwich, *Revelations of Divine Love*, translated by Clifton Wolters (Penguin Classics, 1966; copyright © Clifton Wolters, 1966).

John Reilly: *Crucifixion* (front cover). 34 Madeira Road, Ventnor, Isle of Wight PO38 1HW.

Introduction

> After breakfast, Jesus said to Simon Peter, 'Simon son of John, do you love me more than all else?' 'Yes, Lord,' he answered, 'you know that I love you.' 'Then feed my lambs', he said. A second time he asked, 'Simon son of John, do you love me?' 'Yes, Lord, you know I love you.' 'Then tend my sheep.' A third time he said, 'Simon, son of John, do you love me?' Peter was hurt that he asked him a third time, 'Do you love me?' 'Lord,' he said, 'you know everything; you know I love you.' Jesus said, 'Feed my sheep.' (John 21, 15-17; NEB)

One of the most recurring features of the life of young people today is a searching and a yearning for something deeper and more fulfilling than the endless demands of consumerism and materialism. Since its foundation in 1811, the National Society has been committed to trying to provide children with just such a foundation, based on the teaching and practices of the Church of England. One of its earliest logos has the words 'Feed my sheep' on it. In line with this the society has always been in the forefront of educational practice, searching for ways in which to help children come to a deeper understanding of the truth of the gospel.

Part of modern culture is the ever-present visual image. Books are almost always illustrated, magazines and newspapers carry colour pictures and television dominates everywhere. Film and video record every aspect of life while hoardings and advertisements use the image, sometimes with frightening irresponsibility, to sell goods. Pictures are used to decorate everyday objects, such as the mouse-mat for the computer or the biscuit tin and last, but by no means least, artists continue to paint and draw, to sculpt and build, and to use modern methods to convey timeless ideas through modern techniques such as video installations. Is the image, therefore, just a useful tool, a source of inspiration, a challenging medium, or is it something which needs also to be understood, used with caution and put before children with a good deal of careful explanation?

The chicken in the corner

One teacher, Frances Moffatt, told me of an incident that occurred early in her own teaching career. She had been inspired one Christmas to prepare the children in her primary class for the event by showing them a large painting of a nativity scene, full of colour and incident. She talked through the story with the children using the various parts of the painting to illustrate the story of the birth of Christ, the shepherds, the angels and the wise men. The children listened intently and she thought they had learnt something until she stopped speaking and one small boy shot his hand into the air: 'Please, miss,' he said 'what is the chicken in the corner doing?' This was in rural Ireland, and Frances realized that angels and wise men were a long way from this child's knowledge, but chickens – well that was another story and far closer to what interested him. Frances recognized, as a young teacher, that you had to touch children at a point which tallied with their real experience, not what the teacher imagined they might be interested in considering.

It was this story which led to my decision, after some eight years in parish ministry, to go to Birkbeck College, University of London, to study for a BA in the History of Art, followed later by an MA in Arts Education at the University of Warwick. During these years of study I have realized the enormous power of art both to illuminate and inspire and to confuse and destroy. It is the intention of this book not to tell teachers how art should be used, but to introduce different aspects of art and art history in such a way that teachers can use the potential of this visual medium in their work in religious education and avoid some of the pitfalls.

Implicit within the command to 'feed his sheep' is the concept of nourishment. We feed children in order that their bodies may be properly nourished so that they grow into normal adulthood. Within the field of religious education there is the vital food which is simply information: information about the Christian faith, its history, the life of its founder and the development of the Church. Then there is the more general nourishment in the form of spiritual development and awareness, coupled with the knowledge of worship and ritual. In the history of art both these types of nourishment have been taken from images. They have been used as 'the books of the illiterate' and as inspiration for meditation and worship. They have also been used for far more materialistic purposes to enhance the prestige of the patron and, indeed, the artist. The question facing teachers today is whether or not, in the late twentieth century, it is still valid to try and use images to impart information and to inspire devotion. In this equation, the materialistic cannot be ignored.

Art and inspiration

What marked out the life of Jesus Christ was his ability to inspire all those with whom he had contact to turn towards God. Time and again as he reached out to the poor and the suffering and to his disciples, he used his power to connect that individual to the strength of God's love. Today, at the touch of a computer key, we can be connected to the Internet and, potentially, in touch with ideas and people all over the world. We communicate with other people with the greatest of ease, we exchange views and learn about each other. Yet, at the same time, we live in a society which has simply lost the ability to connect with the spiritual and is largely unaware that the love of God is closer to us than all those Web sites and can be accessed far more quickly than any computer. What is, perhaps, missing is the inspiration which turns religion from something boring and unwanted into the source of all life.

During his life on earth, Jesus Christ took his parables from the world around him. He did not reject all that was in the world, but told us to use everything to the glory of God. The visual image is an overpowering presence in our lives today. We cannot escape from it. So it is perhaps very important that the RE teacher knows how to use images in the service of God, to inspire children to explore his love and learn more of his works.

Part 1

Religious Education and the Practice of Art History

1

Religious Education and Art: Art and Religious Education

Some reasons for the links and a discussion of attitudes to art

What is 'art'?

What is 'art'? We all like to think we understand the meaning of the term, but it is, in fact, not so easy. The Pan *Dictionary*, a lively modern dictionary, published in 1979, describes it as:

> any objects or activities in which man expresses feelings and ideas about life by giving them some imaginative form.

On the other hand, the Odhams *Dictionary*, of a more classical vein and published in 1946 says:

> a craft or skill employed by man to do or make a thing, or to produce or improve a quality; skill or aptitude in aesthetics or in certain crafts; a branch of aesthetics itself; the organized general principles of many crafts, sciences and activities; cunning skills in deception, a person's skill and sublety generally; (pl) occupations requiring sensibility, ingenuity, or intellect, primarily the fine arts such as poetry, painting sculpture, music, architecture; secondarily the useful arts as of manufacture or the household etc., third the purely intellectual arts such as mathematics, dialectics, pure chemistry, etc.

How do we *interpret* a work of art?

With a subject so diffuse, great challenges arise for the teacher because, lying behind the understanding of what we mean by 'art', is the even more vexing question of interpretation. It is this question that will lie behind the approach of this book. It is from the way in which we *interpret* an object or building, music or literature that our aesthetic appreciation comes. The work of the teacher, therefore, must be to help pupils through to an interpretation which allows them to appreciate the arts for themselves. This will help pupils to see all the possibilities and have the freedom to accept or reject from within their own understanding and experience. From the outset the teacher needs to be aware of the temptation to impose his or her own viewpoint on the pupil and to avoid doing that wherever possible. A simple example of a toddler's first steps in the world of art will explain this:

> I decided to send my eighteen-month old grandson an Easter card and, as was the tradition in my family, I drew a little picture of myself – a pin face with a big smile – at the end. At least, I thought I was drawing myself sending a smile to my grandson, but when my daughter showed him the card, he took one look and promptly added another word to his growing vocabulary: 'Man' he said, triumphantly. Now he knew the card was from Granny who was quite definitely not a man but he had interpreted the picture as one of himself, whom he knew to be 'man'.

So there, with something as simple as a pin-face, we have a difference of interpretation. If the teacher can accept this – the enormous power of art to link in at many different levels to different individuals – and approach the subject as one who is opening doors and widening horizons, then the complexities of the subject become an adventure into the unknown and not a journey through a thicket of problems.

This is particularly important when dealing with issues relating to religious art, and Christian art in particular. For a long time the question of whether it is right or wrong to use art in the service of religion has been a subject of debate throughout the world. If pupils are to move beyond the use of religious images as illustration to understand their position in the living practice of different faiths, they will need to enter into the mind-set of the various faiths in such a way as to be able to assess the significance of the art or artefacts. This need not be difficult and, if individual pupils' religious faith is respected, good work can result.

Art and culture

Christian art cannot be separated from the cultures in which it is produced, nor from the secular art which surrounds it. Most artists work in more than one style, more than one medium and cover a wide variety of subjects. It is impossible to introduce children to Christian images without introducing them also to the more secular images. Again this can be used positively and seen as a chance to explore issues which need addressing. The only caveat is that teachers need to be aware at the outset, that most good art history books cover the whole gamut of production by any one artist or period and so such books will contain a number of images which need to be treated carefully, with thought for the age group being taught.

Art and values

This is the challenge and the opportunity for the skilled teacher: art in all its many forms addresses all the great issues of life. If teachers can help pupils, through an appreciation of art, to consider some of these issues, then perhaps the whole curriculum will be enhanced. It is particularly important for the RE teacher to work with pupils to address some of the issues raised by the use of images in a world where the image has become a dominating force throughout the media. The role of the paparazzi in the life and tragic death of the Princess of Wales is just one example of the increased power of the photographic image in our society. However, this is not really new. Powerful rulers and leaders have always understood the power of the image to create a statement about their position and often used various forms of religious art to emphasize this.

Right and wrong in art

One of the subjects about which there is much discussion at the moment, is the problem of how to give pupils an ethical framework to help them cope with the problems and temptations that surround them in a plural society where different groups have different ideas of the correct way to behave. A study of the history of art within Religious Education can help pupils to debate and consider issues of morality in a way which allows them the freedom to begin to formulate their own codes in relation to their particular family background.

It is the aim of this book to help teachers with this sort of problem and to show how even difficult modern art can be used to help pupils with an exploration of ethical issues. It will address the questions of beliefs and values. This, of course, must include the question of the differing attitudes of different cultural groups to artistic questions in both religious art and what is known as secular art. Although reference will be made in the discussion to the art of different religions, the main emphasis in this book will be on Western art, which necessarily has as its basis the Christian cultural background.

What is religious art?

What constitutes religious art? Clearly a picture of the crucifixion of Christ is an image directly related to one of the key events of the Christian story and can be called *Christian* art. But is a photographic image which tells us of the suffering and starvation in a country undergoing a drought unconnected to Christian ideas? This raises the whole question of the motive of the artist, the patron for whom he or she is working and the response of the viewer. Within the context of religious education, clearly almost any image can be used to develop discussion about the world in which we live and the ideas we formulate to help us with that living. It is, therefore, important for the teacher to be able to distinguish the different types of art and to set them in context for the pupils as part of that discussion.

By now there will be those teachers who are groaning at the thought of yet more pressure on an already overcrowded curriculum. How, they will wonder, can these ideas relating to art be added into the tight schedules in a busy classroom? The idea behind this handbook is that art is already present in Religious Education, through the illustrations in books, the decorations in religious buildings and throughout the media. Consider for one moment the mass of Christian images which appear on Christmas cards and sometimes stamps, the covers of CDs and tapes of religious music which are usually decorated with Christian images or symbols and the various images scattered throughout society. These all mean that teachers need to be able to discuss these issues with pupils.

2

The Development of Christian Art in Western Europe

Christian art from the first century AD to modern times

Theological attitudes

The church is dark – richly decorated with mosaics which glitter unevenly in the candlelight. The stained glass glows in the evening sun. Wafts of incense rise to the ceiling and the liturgy flows along, following one of the many rites now practised in Christian churches. The music, rising into the vaulted ceiling, is a mixture of a classical setting for a mass and modern hymns. The church was built in the middle of the nineteenth century by Pugin. The glass was made by the William Morris workshop to a design by Dante Gabriel Rossetti. The vestments, curiously, do not blend. They are the vibrant work of a modern embroiderer, using symbol and colour to carry forward the message. They seem to dominate the softer colour of the altar frontal with its symbolism of the Holy Spirit. The Mothers' Union banner, made at the beginning of this century to a design by Margaret Tarrant, seems faded and the soft contours of the Madonna's face are almost lost. The altarpiece recedes into the darkness – the work of a seventeenth-century Spanish Catholic artist, it arrived in England from the spoils of the Grand Tour. It moved from a stately home gallery to this church as the gift of the patron after the Oxford Movement had allowed an explosion of art in all its forms back into the former simplicity of the Church of England, largely free from images in its churches.

At much the same moment, in a small village, deep in rural England, Evensong is being said by the churchwarden for a small group of parishioners. This church, a Norman building with some Victorian additions by way of a porch and a side aisle, is still a plain stone building. The walls between plain windows and pillars are whitewashed. The only colour is in the flowers, the tapestry kneelers which use various symbols to represent the dedication of the church to St Paul and in a large hanging at the back to keep out the draughts, which represents different aspects of life in the village. The altar is a simple wooden table carved to match the pews. On it rests a plain, brass cross and two candlesticks. Apart from the thin sound of the opening hymn, the only music is the lilting cadence of Cranmer's English, carefully rendered by the churchwarden and his congregation.

These two imaginary descriptions could be true and serve to point up the importance, when introducing Christian art to children today, of realizing the very complex background and history to the current situation.

Early Christian images

It is not known precisely how early Christian representational art developed, although at a fairly early stage Christians began to gather in specific buildings, thus beginning the long tradition of Christian architecture. Scholars debate the issue of whether or not the very early Church condemned or encouraged the use of images. Despite the increasing amount of speculative 'theology' which is now being published about the early years of Christianity and the position of Jesus, it does seem certain that the first Christians were Jewish. It is unlikely, therefore, coming from that tradition, that they would have thought to make images to represent their doctrinal ideas.

Christian images in the Roman Empire

It is possible that it was when Christianity began to spread from its Palestinian roots across the Roman Empire that the use of images became more acceptable. Evidence of the wall-paintings in the synagogue at Dura Europos is used to argue that Christians may have decorated their buildings earlier than previously thought. However, no specifically Christian buildings survive from that date. The Romans, following on from and adapting Greek traditions of art, added to them ideas gathered from different parts of their Empire. They used images in many ways including pagan ritual and emperor worship.

The earliest known Christian images date from between about AD 250 to 400 and are to be found in the catacombs in Rome. These images arouse debate because, while some of them have a clear Christian symbolism, others are more ambiguous. One of these is a Good Shepherd image, often found in modern RE textbooks. The interesting point about this early image, if it is indeed meant to represent Jesus, is that the figure wears Roman dress and is beardless. In other words, it does not conform to the 'standard' image of Jesus with long hair, a beard, staring eyes and a long nose, which originated in Byzantine art. This latter image is said to derive from the Mandylion of Edessa, a cloth reputedly imprinted by Jesus with a likeness of his face and sent by him to the king of Edessa (in modern Syria). In Western art it is connected with the legend that an image was left on the cloth pressed to Jesus' face by Veronica on his way to Calvary or with the tradition that St Luke was a painter and painted the archetype of the image of Jesus. The origins of all these legends are lost in medieval mythology and are very difficult to verify.

The spread of Christian imagery across Europe

During the fourth century Christianity became established as the official religion of the Roman Empire, and Christian images began to be used in a variety of ways. Churches were built and then decorated with wall-paintings and mosaics. Tombs carried complex programmes of sculpture and individual sculptures found a place in homes and churches. Architecture developed from simple hall churches to the great basilicas such as Hagia Sophia in Constantinople, built between AD 532 and AD 537. The city of Rome also posesses a rich concentration of churches, mosaics and sculptures from this period. As Christian missionaries spread across Europe, carrying the gospel message, they took with them books written on vellum which were sometimes richly illuminated (illustrated) with miniature paintings and drawings. The earliest of these have not survived but there are many examples from the seventh century onwards. There were also small ivories, decorated church plate, reliquaries and rich, embroidered vestments (these last have only survived from a slightly later period). Thus, by the time Islam became influential in the seventh century AD, the use of the painted, sculpted or mosaic image as an expression of Christian belief, was widespread.

The development of images of Christ

During the early Christian era, a lamb was often used to symbolize Jesus as 'the Lamb of God' (as in John 1.29). By the seventh century, Christian art had moved away from this symbolic representation of Jesus as 'The Lamb', to one where, generally, the image was a naturalistic representation of the human form of Jesus.

The arguments of this period derived directly from all the earlier debates prior to the Council of Nicaea in AD 325, about what exactly was meant by the doctrine of the Incarnation. Put very simply, the problem was that, if Jesus, as man, was also fully God, then since God could not be depicted neither could Jesus be. The argument for God never being depicted originates in the Jewish concept that Yahweh was beyond representation; hence the prohibition in the second commandment, 'You shall not make for yourself any idol. God is spirit, and those who worship him must worship in spirit and in truth' (*The Alternative Service Book 1980*). The Christological debates around the use of images are very complex but it is worth grasping the essence of them because they continue right up to the present day and have generated a vast literature.

Early iconoclasm

The impact of the Muslim prohibition on the use of images of God undoubtedly had an impact on the Byzantine world, and the first major wave of iconoclasm began in 730, when Emperor Leo III ordered the destruction of images which showed Jesus, the Virgin Mary and other Christian figures in human form. The iconoclast controversy raged on for much of the eight and ninth centuries, despite the restoration of images by the Byzantine Church following the second council of Nicaea in 787. In the Western Church Pope Gregory II (Pope 999–1003) endorsed the use of images as 'the books of the illiterate'.

After this period images continued to be used in both East and West, but it was a debate which never really disappeared. The Lollards, followers of John Wyclif in England at the end of the fourteenth century and into the early fifteenth century, preached against the use of images. There was a growing groundswell throughout Europe during this period that the Roman Catholic Church was corrupt and that the use of images was part of this corruption.

The Reformation

It was, of course, with that explosion of writing and thinking known as the Reformation that the iconoclastic controversy erupted again with violence. Luther's broad-minded tolerance was not copied by his followers and, in the 1520s there was wholesale destruction of images. Calvin added to the wave of destruction when, in 1536, he published the first edition of *The Institutes of the Christian Religion*, which condemned the use of religious images. With the logic of a trained lawyer, he pointed out that you cannot make an image of that 'which you cannot see'. From that moment, the development of the history of art followed two distinct lines: on the one hand were the images deriving from or depicting secular life and on the other those which continued to be made for Christian practice, mainly for the Orthodox and Roman Catholic Churches.

The development of secular art in western Europe received a tremendous boost as patrons still wanted pictures to decorate their homes and meeting places. Despite the ruling of the Council of Trent in AD 1563 that the use of images was acceptable, provided they were suitable, Protestant groups never again used images in quite the same way. Some modern writers are arguing that the loss of their images was forced onto the English people by an intolerant series of Protestant governments. However, although no doubt many were distressed by the iconoclasm of the sixteenth and seventeenth centuries, it is clear that after the Act of Uniformity of 1662, the majority of members of the Protestant Churches were happy to worship and study without the aid of images. Within the Roman Catholic and Orthodox worlds, images continued to be produced, following closely on established conventions and under the strict control of the Church.

Late developments

In 1829 the House of Commons passed the Act of Catholic Emancipation. This was followed, over the next twenty years, by the development of the Oxford Movement, an Anglo-Catholic revival movement. These two events combined to create an explosion of church building for both Roman Catholics and Anglo-Catholics during the nineteenth century. These buildings included images, in their stained glass, their church furnishings, altarpieces, vestments and plate. For the first time, since the Reformation, English artists were able to work for their home market in this field. The imaginary church in the first description at the beginning of this snapshot outline of the ebb and flow of Christian art lies within this revival period.

The current position

The position today is very varied. Even within the Church of England, there are those who still hold fast to the idea that the use of images during worship and in Christian practice is wrong, while others are developing ideas about Christian art which are very close to those of the Roman Catholic or the Orthodox Church, both of which have their individual viewpoints. It is interesting to note, however, that within mainstream Church of England practice, the use of Christian imagery is primarily decorative and it is not often incorporated into ritual and practice.

3

The Development of Styles in the Art of Western Europe

An outline of the main periods of Western art, with particular reference to Christian art

Art and the National Curriculum

The history of art as an academic discipline is relatively new. Before the end of the last century, the subject was mostly included within such subjects as history or art; indeed modern courses in history and art still expect students to learn about various cultural aspects of the period under study. The National Curriculum for Art for Key Stages 2 and 3, in particular, expects that:

> Pupils should be introduced to the work of artists, craftspeople and designers, eg *drawing, painting, printmaking, photography, sculpture, ceramics, textiles, graphic design, architecture*, in order to develop their appreciation of the richness of our diverse cultural heritage.

The National Curriculum for History for Key Stages 2 and 3 states that children should be taught:

> history from a variety of perspectives – political; economic, technological and scientific; social; religious; cultural and aesthetic.

The National Curriculum for History, under the heading of Key Elements at Key Stage 2, states that:

Pupils should be taught:

a) to place the events, people and changes in the periods studied within a chronological framework;

b) to use dates and terms relating to the passing of time, including ancient, modern, BC, AD, century and decade [note: there is no mention of the more modern use of CE, Common Era], and terms that define different periods, e.g. *Tudor, Victorian.*

For Key Stage 3, the same section states:

> Pupils should be taught:
>
> a) to place the events, people and changes in the periods studied within a chronological framework;
>
> b) to use dates, terms and conventions that describe historical periods and the passing of time, e.g. *era, medieval, Reformation, Industrial Revolution, Hanoverian, Georgian.*

Within the Key Stage 3 National Curriculum for Art, you find that:

> The Western tradition should be exemplified by works chosen from Classical and Medieval, Renaissance and post-Renaissance periods through to the nineteenth and twentieth centuries. Works selected from non-Western cultures should exemplify a range of traditions from different times and places.

From this two facts become clear: first, that pupils in the RE classroom and, indeed the science classrooms will be there with at least a basic grounding in some of the history of art; second, that they will have acquired a 'labelling' system which attempts to divide the sweep of history into manageable periods. The trouble is that periods do not always tally within different subjects. For example what in history and the history of art is described as 'the Renaissance' is also the period of 'the Reformation'. This section will describe the main terms used by art historians to describe different periods. However, teachers would be well-advised to consult one or more of the books which give lists of art terms and other references. Within the RE classroom it might be much more helpful to stick to a simple dating system which will not add to the confusion for Key Stages 2 and 3, where the pupils can only have acquired a skeleton grounding from the History and Art curricula. For example, if the teacher wishes to show pupils an image from a medieval period, it would be better to say this is an image from say, AD 750, rather than to cause confusion with the use of such terms as 'Byzantine'. This use of a straightforward dating system will also avoid the problem that in a multi-ethnic class, different groups of children may be used to considering, in terms of their religion, different periods under different headings.

Another reason for presenting images to pupils with as little 'labelling' as possible is that in art history, as with many disciplines, there are vogues and fashions for describing periods of art or particular styles and designs in a particular way. Within the art classroom, pupils should be given some familiarity with all these terms, but from the viewpoint of RE it will be much easier if the pupils consider the images free from such 'labels' which at some periods have been used in a pejorative way. This underlines the purpose of using art in the RE classroom. It is to use the vibrant ideas created by artists and architects to help open up the pupils' understanding of the wonder of God's creation and the diversity, beauty and complexity of the world. The following list of terms, therefore, is given to help RE teachers to find their way through the literature and to decide how best to follow a course of reading to help with their particular responsibilities. This is necessary because many art history books carry one of these terms as a title.

Art history periods

These periods have been selected to give teachers a broad idea of the main headings under which art history is, or has been, discussed. It is not intended to be comprehensive and, if teachers find themselves confused by a particular term not mentioned here, they are recommended to consult one of the reference books listed in the Appendix.

As in all subjects, the terminology used in the history of art is subject to change, both from a technical angle and from the way objects are assessed. Teachers will find that art history books from different periods may well view an object or building from quite different criteria. This need not be a problem and, if pupils find different ideas in their reading and research, this can be used to point out changing attitudes to images.

Classical

'Classical' is normally used to describe a sweep of history in the Greek and Roman worlds from about the fifth century BC to about AD 400. It covers the development of Greek art and then links this to the spread of classical ideas throughout the Roman Empire. In most art history books the period from the fifth to the third century BC in Greece is presented as the apogee of style and form and the Roman developments are often belittled when set beside their Greek antecedents. The term recurs in the fifteenth and sixteenth centuries, when there was a return to the principles of design, order and form which had been laid down by such writers as Vitruvius (first century BC) and as a result of the discovery of much early Greek and Roman sculpture. It also comes back in architectural history in the form of Neo-classicism at the end of the eighteenth century and in the nineteenth century when many public buildings were built from designs drawn from the earlier Greek and Roman periods.

Roman

'Roman' usually refers to the art and architecture of the period from about 200 BC to about AD 400, thus including the main period of the Roman Empire from Julius Caesar to the arrival of the Goths in Europe. The later part of this period obviously overlaps with the early Christian period and books will vary in the label attached, depending on the perspective from which they are written. The Roman period included some of the most amazing engineering feats ever realized, such as the great aqueducts and the huge basilicas and bath houses. The paintings of the period which have now been discovered in places such as Pompeii indicate that the Romans developed many ideas of their own which were not just derived from Greek patterns.

Early Christian

Early Christian art is usually taken to be that of the period from the death and resurrection of Jesus until the main medieval period. Very little is known about Christian art in the first and second centuries, with the first real evidence coming from the catacombs and sarcophagi from about AD 250. This overlaps with the Roman period, and the early Christian images show a clear link with late Roman styles. There is considerable debate about the extent of early Christian art, and perceptions of this period which may well change its history as archaeology is extended and theology explored, but clearly the attitude of the early Church has an important bearing on the debates of the Reformation in the sixteenth century and on the nineteenth and twentieth centuries in England.

Byzantine

While the Roman Catholic Church dominated western Europe until the sixteenth century, from the sixth century there was an increasing split between the Church in the East and in the West, culminating in the so-called Great Schism of 1054. The word 'Byzantine' comes from the fact that the city of Constantinople was founded on the site of the ancient city of Byzantium, and the term is used in the history of art to describe the religious images and distinctive architecture of the Eastern Church. During the early medieval period, many images, even in the West, were influenced by this style. One of the first indications of the beginnings of the Renaissance was the move by artists, such as Giotto (c. 1267–1337), to shift away from this style to a more naturalistic one.

Medieval

This period is often referred to as 'the Middle Ages' in history books, but in art history the preferred term is 'the medieval period'. 'Medieval' can be used to describe anything from AD 300/400 up to the end of the fourteenth century. (Some art of this last century may be described as International Gothic or Early Renaissance – see below). It is a very important period in the history of art because it saw a huge flowering of Christian imagery and architecture and the development of the use of art in Christian worship in a number of ways. Despite the period of iconoclasm in the East during the eighth century, the use of images became an assured and potent part of Christian life. This period was the one to which the mid- and late Victorian artists in England turned for inspiration and, just as the Greek classical ideas were revamped later, so the medieval ideas inspired the Gothic Revival (see below).

Dark Ages

This phrase is sometimes used to describe the medieval period between about AD 500 and 1100, when there was much confusion in western Europe with invading forces causing widespread devastation. However, although much was destroyed, it is not true to say that there were no great works of art. There are many beautiful manuscripts, ivories, jewellery and other small objects which have survived. This is another period of which the assessment is changing as more is discovered about it from archaeology and from previously unpublished documents.

Romanesque

'Romanesque' is generally thought to cover the art and architecture of western Europe between the tenth and the thirteenth centuries. The term 'Romanesque' was invented by a nineteenth-century French archaeologist because he thought this period of artistic development corresponded with the development of Romance languages from Latin. However, although it is true to say that these centuries saw a huge rise in the number of church buildings, there were a number of different styles during the period. In Britain, for instance, the local variant of Romanesque church architecture is known as Norman. A common trend was the further development of very large buildings, with extensive vaulting, rounded arches and massive towers.

Gothic

The term 'Gothic' is used to describe the great cathedrals which were erected in western Europe between about the twelfth and early sixteenth centuries. As used in Italian by the writer and architect Alberti (1404–72), 'Gothic' was used in a derogatory manner, contrasting the style unfavourably with the new Renaissance buildings. The Gothic cathedrals were huge constructions of stone, with rib vaults stretching higher than ever before, large windows letting in much more light and supported by a system of buttresses. Based on the same structural principles, different styles developed in different countries.

After several centuries, during which it was superseded by Renaissance, Baroque and Neo-classical styles, Gothic enjoyed a revival when both the emancipated Roman Catholic Church in

England and the Anglo-Catholic movement, inspired by Pugin began constructing a wave of Victorian neo-Gothic church buildings. The Gothic Revival movement was fuelled by the ideas of the pre-Raphaelites (see below) and the writings of John Ruskin.

International Gothic or International Style

As the Middle Ages drew to a close, some of the courts in places such as France, Burgundy and Italy began to develop a highly sophisticated way of life which encouraged the production of very beautiful artefacts such as books of hours. The particularly elegant style of painting, manuscript illumination and sculpture that evolved at this time has traditionally been called International Gothic. (It is not a term used in architecture.) Recently this has also been called 'the international courtly style'. This period in art is significant because it encouraged the emergence of artists with superb technical skills who paved the way for the great flowering of art in the Renaissance. It was, for example, the period which saw the emergence of the technique of oil painting in northern Europe which enabled painters to create ever more realistic effects.

Renaissance

In art history the term 'Renaissance' comes from the Italian word 'Rinascimento', meaning 'rebirth'. It is usually taken to refer to the period from the fourteenth to the sixteenth century. The great flowering of art in the latter part of this period, spanned by the careers of Leonardo da Vinci, Raphael and Michelangelo, is sometimes designated 'the High Renaissance'. The Renaissance saw a return to classical ideas of form and composition, with the new sciences of perspective and colour being used to create illusionistic effects.

During this period artists flourished because of the vast amount of work available as patrons of all sorts competed to commission the most magnificent works of art, using them as statements of their power and wealth. Despite the protestations of the monk Savonarola at the end of the fifteenth century, the production of works of art during the period continued unabated. New techniques such as oil painting were used with ever-increasing skill to create paintings which were not only beautiful but realistic. Artists increasingly used preliminary drawings taken from life to help them create these effects, and a number of treatises on technique, such as those by Alberti, were published. Sculptors also created works of outstanding beauty. Although the great masters Leonardo da Vinci, Raphael and Michelangelo are still always used in modern textbooks to illustrate the period, many of the so-called minor artists were also men of genius, and, put together, they have inspired generations of people with their paintings, sculpture and architecture.

Reformation

The Reformation is traditionally seen as beginning with the work of Erasmus, brought to a climax by Luther in 1517: 'Erasmus laid the egg that Luther hatched' is often quoted by historians. No less significant were the several editions of *The Institutes of the Christian Religion* by John Calvin. However, the development of the Reformation was very complex, and there had been a series of movements throughout Europe since the eleventh century which had tried to effect changes in the mores of the Roman Catholic Church. The monastic orders of the Franciscans and the Cistercians both preached against excessive luxury and wealth. John Wyclif and the Lollards in England at the end of the fourteenth century and the Brethren of the Common Life in France and Germany during the fifteenth century all helped to create the atmosphere in which the dramatic events of the sixteenth century could take place. Artistic, literary and practical developments, such as the invention of movable type, which allowed books to be much more readily available, also had their part to play in creating the explosion of activity which took place in all the arts from about 1400 until the conclusion of the Council of Trent in 1563.

Mannerism

The term 'Mannerism' developed from the use by the sixteenth-century writer Vasari, in his *Lives of the Artists*, of the Italian word *maniera* to describe the new and much more dramatic way in which artists were painting from about 1520 onwards. If the work of Piero della Francsca is contrasted with that of Parmigianino, then the comparison is clear. It was a style which, from the outset attracted both praise and criticism. It led on naturally to the *Baroque* (see below). Due to our modern tendency to regard someone whose behaviour is *mannered* as unpleasant, this is one of those terms which needs to be treated with caution if pupils are not to misinterpret it and, therefore, possibly not be open to some of the outstanding examples of painting and sculpture produced during the sixteenth century, both before and after the Council of Trent. Like several other terms, it is also one which is beginning to be used less by art historians working in that period.

Baroque

The Baroque period runs from the end of the sixteenth century and on through the seventeenth century. It was a much more dramatic style, with both paintings and sculptures full of colour and movement. An example of baroque painting is the highly illusionistic ceiling in the church of Gésu in Rome or the painted churches built in Germany during the seventeenth century. Painters introduced fantastic programmes of images which incorporated every sort of perspectival trick to create a sense of overpowering reality. Architects responded by moving on from the more classical styles of building of the Renaissance to create buildings which were full of colour and decoration. A point to note is that the term 'baroque' is used in art history about a century before the same term was applied to music. Again, this is a term which is now applied with some caution, and books about this period may well simply refer to the seventeenth century.

Enlightenment

With the dawn of the eighteenth century, there came an explosion of new ideas which gradually eroded the grip of Christian theology on patterns of thinking. Freed from the control of the Roman Catholic Church, thinkers throughout the Protestant countries of Europe began to explore new and revolutionary ways of explaining the meaning of the universe. This term is more often used in history books. Art history books of the same period will tend to be described as about the eighteenth century, although in the text references will often be made to this period of thinking.

Victorian

It might seem unnecessary to include this term. In general it is, of course, the period of the reign of Queen Victoria and applicable only in Britain. However, in both art history writing and in design, it became a term of abuse, used to describe what was considered boring, banal and overly-sentimental. This was due in part to some of the more modern movements such as *Impressionism* (see below) and the social and artistic developments since the Second World War.

Recently there has been a shift in opinion, and art from this period which stuck to a conventional style and did not follow the modern movements, is being taken much more seriously for both its artistic and its social merits. For example, Frith, once dismissed as 'sentimental', is now being seen as a good recorder of the social mores of the time, and his artistic skill is receiving due respect. There are many Victorian paintings which depict aspects of life in that period which could help pupils to explore the context of some of the great Christian reformers of the time, such as Lord Shaftesbury, William Wilberforce and Josephine Butler.

Pre-Raphaelite

The Pre-Raphaelite Brotherhood was formed in the 1850s, and its stated aim was to return art to the standards and styles of the period before the work of the Renaissance artist, Raphael. Their work coincided with the return to the idea of the medieval period as the ideal one, both in terms of the life of the Church and in terms of artistic excellence. Strictly speaking, this term describes a style and a movement in British art, rather than a period, but it has come also to mean a particular period of the mid- to late Victorian era. For a long time the Pre-Raphaelites were written off as eccentric and unattractive by these critics who were influenced by the developments in Impressionism and the more modern periods. However, recently there has been a great revival of interest in their work with their style of painting being recognized as a significant influence on some later painters.

Impressionism

This is a term coined in France to describe the new and revolutionary style used by a group of painters who broke away from the conventions of the French Academy in the mid- to late nineteenth century to experiment with colour, light, form and composition and create quite new effects. This new style released artists from the strict control of the Academics, who set the categories of paintings and the technical standards for works to be displayed in their exhibitions. However the term has also come to be used to describe a particular period of art. It is interesting that it overlaps with the period of the Pre-Raphaelites and with the period of conventional Victorian painting. There were also British Impressionists who worked in a tradition begun by J.M.W. Turner (1775–1851) who is often described as the forerunner of Impressionism.

Modern periods

From the beginning of the twentieth century, artistic style after artistic style has appeared with ever- increasing rapidity. The art scene which has seen Cubism, Fauvism, Dadaism, Surrealism, Expressionism, post-expressionism, to name just a few, is now crowded with a huge variety of styles. Teachers who would like to use material from the twentieth century would be advised to read one of the good introductions to the period and then make a careful selection to show children. Modern and postmodern art have some innovative ideas, mainly in the use of technique. However, it is surprising how often the basic idea comes straight from one of the earliest periods. For example, the work of Damien Hirst in placing dissected animals in formaldehyde is merely following on from examples of Dutch art where butchers' shops are shown in great detail or from the anatomical drawings of Leonardo da Vinci, who was no stranger to the abbatoir and the dissecting room.

Art from other cultures

The terms given above relate strictly to the way European and North American art are described. Chinese art, South American art, African art, Australian and New Zealand aboriginal art, for example, all have their own descriptive chronologies. Courses on art from different cultures are often available in extra-mural departments of universities, and teachers who would like to extend their knowledge of one particular culture – perhaps because there are a number of children from that culture in their school – are advised to try and attend such a course. This will give an insight not only into the art of the country concerned but also into the way that that culture relates to religious ideas.

4

Symbols and Ideas in Art

Introduction to iconography and some of the main subjects of Christian painting

Making ideas visible

> After this I saw with my own eyes in the face of the crucifix hanging before me and at which I was ceaselessly gazing something of his passion. I saw insults and spittle and disfiguring and bruising, and lingering pain more than I know how to describe: and there were frequent changes of colour. On one occasion I saw that half his face, from side to centre, was covered with dry blood, and that afterwards the other half similarly was covered, the first half clearing as the second came.
>
> All this I saw physically, yet obscurely and mysteriously. But I wanted to see it even more vividly and clearly. To my mind came the answer, 'If God wills to show you more, he will be your light. You need none but him.'
>
> From *Revelations of Divine Love*, The second revelation.
> Mother Julian of Norwich

At the beginning of Chapter 1 we asked the question, 'what is art?' This chapter asks what can art do or not do? How far can art be more than just a visible expression of an inner idea? Can it represent truth or tell us things which we would otherwise not understand? In the extract from Mother Julian's writings given above we find her looking for visual confirmation of the presence of God. She received the visions which inspired these words in 1373 and it is not surprising that the descriptive language she used is very close to some of the paintings of the crucifixion around at that time. That is not said to invalidate the quality of her insights into the nature of God, but it does just indicate the extent to which what we have seen expressed in paint and stone can have a powerful effect on the way we interpret ideas of God.

It is a very modern book, *Mister God This is Anna*, by 'Fynn' written six hundred years after Mother Julian, which gives us an insight into some of the problems surrounding the question of whether or not doctrinal ideas can be effectively visualized. Fynn and Anna settle down to one of their discussions, and Anna begins to draw her idea of the universe on the pavement, starting with a circle:

> 'That', she said, 'is that there', and she pointed to a dot outside the circle and marked it with a cross. Then, pointing to a dot inside the circle, she said 'That is that dot outside the circle, and that is the tree', and with her finger on the 'tree dot' inside the circle, she continued with, 'And that's the tree inside me.'
>
> 'I seem to have been here before', I [Fynn] murmured.
>
> 'And that', she exclaimed in triumph, laying her finger on a dot inside the circle, 'is a – is a – a flying elephant. But where is it outside? Where is it Fynn?'
>
> 'There ain't no such beastie, so it can't be outside,' I explained.
>
> 'Well then, how did it get into my head?' She sat back on her heels and stared at me.
>
> 'How anything gets into your head beats me, but a flying elephant is pure imagination, it's not factual.'

> 'Ain't my imagination a fact, Fynn?' she quizzed me with a tilt of her head.
>
> 'Sure, of course your imagination is a fact, but what comes out of it isn't necessarily a fact.'
>
> I was beginning to wriggle a bit.
>
> 'Well then, how did it get in there' – she thumped the inside of the circle – 'if it ain't out there' she went on with a few more thumps, 'where did it come from?'

This discussion continues as Anna tries to work out what is coming from within her and what is outside her consciousness. Then the local policeman arrives, to complain about the drawing on the pavement. As he stands on part of the picture, Anna says:

> 'That ain't a picture, mister . . . it's really Mister God. That's me, that's inside me and that's outside me, but it's all Mister God.'

The policeman continues to point out the illegality of their actions, while Anna tries to stop him standing on her picture and Fynn remarks to the policeman:

> 'You've just flattened a couple of billion stars'.

What Anna was trying to do, in making her own picture of the universe, was to put into visual form some of the ideas about God which she had been mulling over. Since the earliest days human beings have been trying to make a visual record of the things they saw around them and have then gone on to try and connect the visible with the unseen. This activity has produced some of the most beautiful paintings and sculptures from a great variety of cultures. Whether you are considering the ritual objects from Africa, the solemn, quiet presence of a Buddha, the lively, dancing images from the Hindu faith or the great range of Christian images, they all have one idea in common and that is to express the inexpressible. They all try to make visible to the general worshipper that overpowering sense of the spiritual presence of 'another' in the world – that quality of human experience which Rudolf Otto described as the 'numinous'.

Iconoclasm: is it still an issue?

Throughout the history of Christianity there has been another view, deriving from the Jewish teaching on the use of imagery in religious practice, that the creating of such visible expressions of the ideas about God is wrong. This has been called iconoclasm. There are two main objections to the use of these images. The first is simply that you cannot make images of things of the imagination and that, therefore, it is better not to try. The second is that images created for this purpose can lead to idolatry and create a situation where the individual's direct access to the love of God is blocked, the image being substituted for the reality.

The image and doctrinal truth

Christians live today in a society where, as scientists unlock the secrets of our DNA and gain an ever-clearer knowledge of the workings of the human body and the brain, many people find it more and more difficult to address the metaphysical and to contemplate the mysteries of faith. Christianity, which is primarily concerned with matters of faith and practice, does not attempt to provide scientific proof for its ideas. This means that the modern technological world, where such scientific proof is axiomatic, the Churches are often found wanting.

Christian art in the classroom

This raises a problem for teachers using Christian art in the classroom. Almost all Christian art is based on the imaginative response of the artist to a commission to provide a picture or sculpture which will visualize some aspect of Christian teaching. Until the advent of the camera in the nineteenth century, even a portrait of a more or less contemporary saint or leader of the church was subject to that indefinable quality of interpretation which takes place as the artist translates memory and idea into plastic form. The images attempting to portray Christ, the disciples and the saints of the early Church are clearly all based on a fiction – sometimes supported by legend and sometimes a new interpretation introduced by an innovative artist. The gospels carry no personal description of Jesus. There is a description in Josephus, a Jewish historian writing in the first century AD, but this is not a first-hand account.

The descriptions in the Bible of the encounter between figures such as Moses and God all indicate a powerful presence but no visible form. Jesus Christ himself, 'looked up to heaven' but no figure appeared. When Jesus spoke of God as 'Abba', he was emphasizing the closeness of his relationship with God, and was using the symbolism of the Fatherhood of God to give us a paradigm of the relationship between God and human beings. Artists have, however, interpreted this by depicting God as an old man with a beard, very often hovering at the top of a painting in 'the heavenly sphere'.

At Christ's baptism we are told that the Holy Spirit descended 'like a dove' or ' in bodily form like a dove'. As a result, the Holy Spirit is always represented in art by a white bird.

When these artistic conventions are understood symbolically, a painting or sculpture can be used to initiate discussion of our ideas of who God might be and the relationship between Father, Son and Holy Spirit. The problem arises in the absence of proper explanation, when children see these images and interpret them literally.

Does imagination have a part to play in RE?

Does this invalidate the use of Christian imagery in the classroom? The answer to this question is simply: 'it depends what the purpose is for the introduction of such images into the RE classroom.' If the purpose of the introduction of art is to give pupils a clear understanding of the history of images in Christian life, then, of course, the more thorough this study can be, the more understanding the pupils will have of a very important part of the history of the Church. This study can, indeed, also make the more dry aspects of Christian history seem more interesting and can encourage pupils to delve a little deeper into the story. If using the art, as suggested in some of the work schemes in Chapter 6, helps pupils to enter into the mind-set of earlier ages, it will do much to help them understand why our ancestors did certain things. It is often by understanding what has brought our society to a certain point that we can begin to cope better with present-day pressures and problems.

Respecting the pupils' own ideas

If the purpose of introducing art is to consider the part of creativity in helping us to understand the power and love of God then this too is perfectly valid. However, the teacher needs to be aware that there are certain pitfalls in this area. One of the main arguments for the use of art in worship and the Christian life is that the sheer beauty of it is uplifting and brings us closer to the glories of creation. Here two very important points need to be borne in mind. First is the question of perception. What the adult considers beautiful, the pupil may very well not understand or even like. Pupils of different ages and different sexes may often view the same work of art from very different viewpoints.

This need not be a problem, provided the teacher understands the psychology of our reaction to images generally and does not try and impose his or her own reaction onto the pupils. Again, it is often only a question of the way in which an image is introduced and a simple statement about an image to be shown, such as: 'You may or may not like this picture, but let's talk about it and consider what you think about it', will free the pupils to judge it from within their own experience.

A further aspect of the question of perception is the fact that images can stir up very powerful reactions in any given pupil quite unexpectedly. The image may touch on some aspect of that pupil's life which is painful or distressing.This need not be a negative, but teachers should consider this aspect of the issue when deciding to introduce a particular image, whether Christian, secular or from another faith's tradition. Teachers working with a class known to them will probably be forewarned of a powerful reaction, but members of education staff in galleries sometimes find themselves confronted with a reaction which is difficult to cope with satisfactorily in that setting. Teachers taking pupils to galleries where some educators now use quite dramatic and lively methods to stir up interest among those pupils need to monitor the situation so that they can, if necessary, pick up the pieces later.

Aesthetics and truth

The last aspect of the question of perception which needs careful preparation is the question of beauty. It has been argued in different ways, over the centuries, that beauty is a revelation of the power and love of God. It is, of course, perfectly true that the ability of the human being to create beauty is one of the marvels of God's creation of the human soul and psyche. However, it is dangerous to move on from this to argue that, therefore, God has a special appreciation of the beautiful. Christianity expressly contains the idea that God's love is for the whole world and that must mean that he sees beauty and ugliness within the same framework of his love. This, of course, is speaking of these attributes in the context of the visual object, not the action. One of the greatest insights of the last hundred years has been the growing recognition of the equal importance in society of the disabled and those whose outer 'looks' do not necessarily conform to a classical standard of beauty. As a society the Western world has begun to legislate against discrimination in all its forms. However, in the world of art the visually ugly has often been used to link the image with evil, and many artists have attempted to portray the good with representations of, say, the physique of Christ, which are as close to perfection as possible.

The teacher can use this dichotomy as a starting point with pupils to explore the whole question of what we mean by beauty and how that fits into the Christian understanding of God's creation. However, when using art as part of this discussion, it is important that the teacher understands the history of the pursuit of the beautiful in religious art in particular and is able to help the pupils place this in context. The link needs to be made with the period in which the art was made and with our modern understanding both of the flaws that can lie beneath the surface of superficial beauty and of the absolute worth, in God's eyes, of all those many people not blessed with such beauty of form.

Can we see God?

In attempting to make the invisible visible, artists have, over the centuries, created many different images which depict God as they imagine Christians think of him. Rooted in the Jewish faith, which has long had a deep suspicion of images of God, the Christian faith has never been able to come to a universally accepted law on images. There are those who see no objection to the artistic interpretation and those who cannot see any purpose in it and even see it as harmful.

The image of God can only be considered from the point of view of whether there is any validity in an imaginary depiction of him. We have no physical description of God, and those descriptions which we do have of encounters with him , such as that of Moses, are only of an overpoweringly strong presence. If God is beyond description, does it matter if we give him an image dressed in human form? This, of course, depends on the theological position of the individual, and some of the theological writing on this subject is extremely convoluted and difficult to follow. Clearly in the average RE classroom, teachers are not going to have the time to tackle these issues in great detail. Yet this issue of exactly what we mean by God is at the heart of many of the doubts facing modern society, which finds it so difficult to accept that which cannot be explained.

The days are long past when people were tortured and put to death for challenging the Church's teaching on such matters. Images which depict doctrines can be used in the classroom to explore such issues and pupils can find the use of such imagery is stimulating.

Images of Jesus – reality or fiction?

Another aspect of this problem – and one which not only exercised the minds of the early church fathers but is also still a subject of debate among scholars – is the question of whether or not Jesus Christ can be properly depicted. The argument starts from the point of whether or not God can be depicted. If the decision is made that he *cannot* be depicted, either because he has never revealed himself in physical form or because any attempt to depict him would be idolatry, then how do you assess the multitude of different images of Jesus Christ? In the credal formulae

Jesus Christ is both God and man – of one substance with God. If this is true, then in his godhead he cannot be depicted – yet in his manhood he clearly had human form like any other. Traditionally artists have coped with this problem by depicting Jesus Christ as a man, but with a halo or other attributes to indicate his divine status. In an age which was used to symbolism, where so much of the world was still a mystery, where science had not attempted to explain away that mystery and where education was not universal, then these artistic formulae were entirely acceptable to most Christians. This did not stop many theologians throughout Western Europe from challenging these norms and questioning the place of images in the Christian faith.

Images of saints

Also contained within the range of Christian religious images are the numerous depictions of the lives of the saints. These have produced some wonderful paintings and sculptures which are full of life and incident. Obviously the extent to which teachers will wish to use these images will depend on their own position on the way in which the saints are to be considered. Again, this is a question of an important Christian doctrine and one which has attracted controversy. The fundamental reason for this is, of course, the extent to which any given saint can be considered able to intercede with God on behalf of the believer. Most of the images created of saints were produced within the context of the intercessionary role of the saints. Today, for most people, they are probably regarded more as role models rather than workers of miracles. However, for the Roman Catholic and Orthodox Churches the position of the saints is still crucial in their life and work. For the teacher, the way in which these images are introduced will, therefore, depend on the school in which they are working.

Thinking through the problems

There are numerous books which give details of the iconography and meaning of the images of the saints and other religious figures. These can help the teacher to explain and clarify the images and provide the basis for a number of interesting lessons, but they do not deal with the fundamental problem of the very different attitudes to the saints. Teachers, therefore, need to think through their own attitudes to this aspect of Christian doctrine and practice, take into account the position of their school and, of course, the likely attitudes of the pupils. Once the teacher is secure in his or her position, then there is no reason why this group of images cannot be used for some important work on the whole question of those outstanding people who have demonstrated the love of God in their lives.

Ideas about the Virgin Mary in art

Ideas surrounding the Virgin Mary have been depicted in another group of images which again touch on doctrines which are not necessarily accepted by all Christians. There are images of her childhood, of her life as the mother of Jesus and of her death – sequences, usually known, when a complete cycle, under the title of *The Life of the Virgin*. Much of this material is based on legendary writings such as the *Golden Legend,* written by Jacobus da Voragine in the thirteenth century. Some of the images, such as *The Assumption of the Virgin Mary*, which depict her rising to heaven and *The Coronation of the Virgin,* which shows Jesus Christ crowning his mother in heaven, are based on doctrines which are not generally accepted within Protestant groups.

Differing attitudes

This outline discussion of some of the images directly linked to different Christian doctrines makes clear that these images will not appeal to all pupils. Some will see them within the context of divine revelation and the teaching authority of the Church. Others will dismiss them as fantasy or the product of misguided ideas. This need not be a problem and, indeed, the very differences of opinion can be used to stimulate work on our different ideas about religious questions and the importance of tolerance and sensitivity when dealing with the views of other people. This is particularly important in the field of images because, to return to the question of perception, for some people the image which represents or symbolizes some very special moment in the development of their own faith can be of the utmost importance.

Is this type of reaction wrong? Is the power of a religious image to evoke deep feelings and strong memories something from which pupils should be protected? Psychologists and psychiatrists may have many arguments for treating the reaction of individuals to images with some caution. However, the fact is that for very many people, a particular religious image can have immense meaning. This facet of religious life needs to be considered in the general teaching about religion, and the careful use of images can help to introduce this subject to pupils.

Chapter 6, which gives advice on linking work with imagery to the National Curriculum, also contains more detail on some of the doctrinal images which occur in art.

Part 2

Teaching Art in RE: RE in Art

5

The National Curriculum and the SCAA/QCA Model Syllabuses in Religious Education

Introduction to ways of linking the National Curriculum in schools and the subject matter of Religious Education

This section aims to demonstrate ways in which the National Curriculum in Art can be linked to the SCAA/QCA Syllabus for Religious Education to enable teachers to explore some of the issues of art and theology within the context of Religious Education. As has been shown in the first part of this book, the history of art is very much part both of the general culture of any society and, in particular, its religious development. If Religious Education is taken out of its pigeonhole and allowed to develop cross-curricular links, then it is likely that pupils will begin to see much more relevance in the subject. This has already been done with some success in the subjects of science and religion, for example, and it is hoped that the ideas in this section will trigger a similar flow of work within the fields of Art and Religious Education. When research was being undertaken on the use of images of Christ, it was clear from the response of pupils at Key Stage 3 that the images themselves were provoking questions, which could lead into a much more lively discussion of the ideas which lay behind the paintings.

The following section gives teachers some pointers as to the way art can be used in the RE classroom in order to help pupils cope with the sometimes complex and demanding problems posed by art. For those teachers who have not studied History of Art in detail, there are suggestions for further reading in the Appendix to this book. This is not a comprehensive guide, but will give teachers a good idea of the basics of the subject.

Art and theory

Every subject carries with it a raft of theory, jargon and interpretation. Often this is far more esoteric and complicated than anything the originator of the object, written work, piece of music or idea had in mind. It is, however, necessary for the teacher to have a grasp of these arguments so that pupils can be prepared to consider the subject from all possible angles. Art history is no exception, and the purpose of this chapter is to introduce teachers who may not be familiar with art theory, to the main ideas. The National Curriculum for Art includes the instruction under the heading of Knowledge and Understanding, for Key Stage 3, that:

> Pupils should be taught to:
>
> a) recognize the diverse methods and approaches used by artists, craftspeople and designers;
>
> b) identify how visual elements are used to convey ideas, feelings and meanings in images and artefacts;
>
> c) relate art, craft and design to its social, historical and cultural context, eg. *identify codes and conventions used in different times and cultures*
>
> d) identify how and why styles and traditions change over time and from place to place, recognizing the contribution of artists, craftspeople and designers;

e) express ideas and opinions and justify preferences, using knowledge and an art, craft and design vocabulary.

At Key Stage 2 similar ground is covered from a simpler point of view. Following this pattern from the curriculum for art, it is possible to demonstrate the way in which art links in to almost every aspect of human life and culture and the way this can be tied into the religious education curriculum.

a) Methods and approaches

One of the most significant features of the artistic temperament is the instinct towards the new, the innovative and the different. Thus we find, for example, that in a period when the techniques of fresco painting, both on wet and dry plaster, had been perfected to a high degree of skill, Leonardo da Vinci decided, when asked to paint a *Last Supper* for the Convent of Santa Maria della Grazie in Milan, to try out a new technique, which incorportated oil and varnish, with the traditional fresco ingredients of egg yolk, pigments and wet plaster. At first this enabled him to produce a luminous depth of painting which demonstrated his interest in the character studies of the disciples. However, it was not a success technically and accounts, in part, for the poor state of the painting now. Many modern artists, likewise, are experimenting with techniques, and conservators, in some cases are facing severe problems in preserving these recent works.

Within the National Curriculum for Art, pupils should be learning about all the main techniques, so that the RE teacher can draw from that to develop a discussion of the way in which our methods and approaches affect our understanding of what we are trying to do. The more skilled we are at a particular technique, the more fluently we can produce an object by that method and then move on to experiment and create something which is new and innovative. The tool we have in our hands affects the way in which we reproduce the image. The lightweight pencil or pen can trace quick, lively lines on the page to convey the immediacy of an idea. Pastels and chalks can, with their dense soft colour, indicate the softness of skin and the velvety finish on a flower petal. Oils can be used, with several oil glazes of one tone over another, to create contrasts of light and shade and a richness of depth and tone, which was lacking from the flatter effect of the earlier egg tempera paintings. The metallic gleam of bronze conveys a different effect of skin and sinew and muscle in a sculpture from that obtained by the patient use of chisel, punch and polish on a block of marble. The use of tubular steel and glass on a modern office block creates a very different sense of the majesty of a large building from that which derives from the arching ribs of stone in a Gothic cathedral.

Art or craft?

At the front of this is the whole question of what is *art* and what is *craft*. At different periods in the history of art, the makers of art have held different roles within the community. Before the fourth century we have very little knowledge of how or why Christian art was produced and we do not know who were the artists who, for example, painted the wall-paintings in the catacombs in Rome or carved the early sarcophagi.

The Middle Ages and workshop practice

From the early Middle Ages until about 1500, all painters, sculptors, masons, architects and craftsmen were organized into guilds, which controlled their work and set standards, rates of pay and conditions of service. At this time, also, almost all art was produced within the context of a busy commercial workshop, which turned out works of art as required by a patron or in order to meet demand for a popular subject, such as the Madonna and Child, which had a ready sale. This accounts for the existence of many different versions of much the same subject. During the sixteenth century artists, particularly painters, sculptors and architects began to break away from their status within the craft guilds and to establish themselves as professional members of the community.

After the Renaissance

Since the Renaissance artists have, increasingly, fashioned an independent lifestyle for themselves. Today, generally, art represents the personal interpretation of a subject by the artist and is not a specific commission by a patron. Obviously, artists who produce a type of image which sells well will be encouraged by the gallery managing them to produce more of the same, but initially the fundamental idea or use of technique will have come from the artist as he or she emerged from art school. This has meant that there is now a huge variety of techniques, some deriving from conventions of the past and some, such as video installations and performance art, which are specifically twentieth century. There is no control over methods used apart from that of commercial success and artists are free to choose a path for themselves.

The one exception to this is, of course, icon-painting where this is done for the Orthodox Churches. This is still undertaken according to prescribed rules and in an atmosphere of prayer to prepare the artist for the task of producing an object which is still very much a part of the living liturgy.

Understanding artistic methods

One way of understanding how people function is to participate in their life to see what it feels like. From a close study of one particular technique from a specific period in the history of art pupils could go on to examine some of the religious ideas of that period within the context of the art which was produced.

The purpose, then, is to explore technique not just from a scientific point of view but also from the social context of the period in order to lead pupils through to a greater understanding of the background to belief. (This can, of course, be linked to section c on page 51)

b) Conveying ideas

Art conveys ideas in three ways:

1. From the purpose as set out by the artist;
2. From the request of the patron;
3. From the deductive response of the viewer which may, or may not, have some relation to the first two purposes.

How does this link to RE work on the conveying of ideas? The primary example might be the search for truth. Artists share one concern with theologians and that is a search for truth. The theologian is generally looking for a way to justify or 'prove' the truth of his or her faith. The artist is generally trying to reproduce an image that has inspired him or her. Artists have many motives for the work they do. Both theologian and artist are, whether they admit it or not, trying to convince or persuade. However, on the whole, the modern artist will have a much more open agenda than the theologian working from a specific religious viewpoint.

In the field of RE the ideas conveyed by images are of a very special nature. As outlined earlier, religious art is necessarily based on the imagination. The lives of all the great men of ideas were, until very recently, unrecorded by photographs, videos or films. Painted and sculpted portraits are always a subjective view of the artist. So there is no real record of the visual side of the Christian story. That does not mean, however, that paintings, sculpture and architecture are devoid of ideas or do nothing to help us understand the great mysteries of the Christian faith. In fact, providing always that the element of imagination is acknowledged, an image can serve as a starting point for the exploration of a great number of doctrinal ideas.

In practical terms, within the Art curriculum, pupils should be receiving insights, at both Key Stages 2 and 3, into the methods used to convey ideas. For example, the way in which colour is used in a painting will determine the way our eyes are drawn to particular features of the painting. Perspective will also draw the eye to a key point. The alignment of figures and the sharpening of one contour over another will make us focus on a particular part of a sculpture. In a Gothic church or cathedral, the glowing colours of the stained glass will focus our eyes on the windows and challenge us to try and work out the stories they depict – or perhaps just to stand and drown in the glory of colour and light so that we reflect on the glory of God, this certainly being one of the purposes of those who built these cathedrals.

When using art to try and develop pupils' interest in the great Christian ideas, it is helpful to divide the various types of Christian art into different sections, because these each have a distinctive function.

Images depicting the life of Jesus Christ and other biblical figures – narratives

If pupils are told, from the outset, that no reliable description of Jesus and other biblical figures exists and that the various images depicting these individuals are based on legend and tradition, then they can see this range of images in the same context as the illustrations to a story book. One way of making this clear, and thus freeing pupils to concentrate on the *point* of the story depicted, is to select a number of different images of Jesus (or any other figure, such as St Peter or St Paul), from different periods and to show them to the class as a group of images. Class discussion can then take place on the different types of image and the reasons for them. If pupils are allowed the freedom to express their own ideas, then such discussions can open up further debate.

Images of Jesus which illustrate the various stories of the gospels, such as the feeding of the five thousand or the Palm Sunday procession or any other moments of the Passion story, can all be used as starting points for teaching pupils those stories and introducing a discussion of the events. This is also an opportunity to amplify the illustrations in textbooks, both by adding to the text and by obtaining larger and better copies of the images used. Alternatively, teachers could arrange a visit to a gallery to see one of the original images or something similar. Provided pupils are told that the image presents the story as it came from the imagination and skills of the artist, then they can go on from there to compare it to the original gospel texts and to discuss different ways of understanding the story.

Images depicting doctrines

These images are more difficult to handle but teachers of Key Stages 2 and 3 need to familiarize themselves with them because they are often used in RE textbooks and usually with very inadequate explanation.

The Trinity

A frequent image is that of the *Trinity*. This comes in three main forms:

1. An image of God as an old man, Christ (usually on a crucifix) and the Holy Spirit as a dove. These need to be distinguished from crucifixion scenes which would come into the narrative section above.)

2. An image of God and Christ as men of a similar age and appearance and the Holy Spirit as a dove.
3. An image of three angels around a table. The most famous example of this type is the early fifteenth century icon by the Russian Orthodox painter Rublev. This is a symbolic interpretation, from within the context of Orthodox theology, of the Old Testament story of Abraham and Sarah and the visit of the three angels in Genesis 18.1-19. The Rublev image omits Abraham and Sarah and just shows the three angels, who are held to be a paradigm of the Trinity.

All these images are difficult to explain to children unless they are reasonably familiar with Christian artistic symbolism but they all appear in Key Stages 2 and 3 books. It would, therefore, be a great help if pupils were prepared for these types of images by having some lessons in the main symbols of Christian art (iconography), perhaps in a brief way at the beginning of each year, which would then enable them to draw more from their textbooks. If good preparatory work is done on symbols, there is no reason why this group of images cannot be used as a starting point for further work on the doctrines of the incarnation and Christological ideas.

The Resurrection, the Ascension and the Transfiguration

The next group of images comprises the *Resurrection*, the *Ascension* and the *Transfiguration*. It is often easy to confuse these images because they tend to show Jesus rising to heaven on a cloud or in a bubble of light known as a *mandorla*. The clue is that in a Resurrection Jesus is usually shown rising out of a tomb, possibly with sleeping soldiers and an angel included in the picture. Ascension scenes usually show Jesus ascending above a group of disciples who are gazing up into the sky. Sometimes this is simply represented by the feet of Jesus at the top of the scene.

This often means that the picture has been cut down at some point, but not always because sometimes only feet were used in confined spaces to indicate the ascent. In the Transfiguration, Jesus is also shown surrounded by light, wearing white and flanked by Moses and Elijah, with the disciples gazing up at him. Most comprehensive books on the Renaissance period will include different examples of these three subjects.

These images need to be treated with great caution in the classroom. The traditional iconography developed during a time when there was no knowledge of space travel, little understanding of the universe and when even the aeroplane was but a speculation in the notebooks of Leonardo da Vinci. The Resurrection is, of course, one of the foundation beliefs of Christianity and is based on narrative accounts of the empty tomb and the appearances of Christ to the women and the disciples. However, the actual event of the Resurrection was never recorded: no one preserved an eye-witness account of how Jesus rose again, and this is one of the mysteries of the Christian faith which must be accepted in the belief in the tradition of the Church that the continued presence of Jesus in the lives of those who turn to him is itself the continuing witness to the truth of the doctrine. There is a danger that pupils will see these artistic impressions from an earlier age, assume that they represent a reality, realize that science and modern travel tell them the image is an impossibility and go on from that to reject Christianity as a foolish and outmoded faith.

How can teachers deal with this problem? There is no simple answer, but much can be done by explaining how these images arose, their context and the world from which they came. If the issue is addressed head on, then teachers can use their very difficulty to begin to explain to pupils the meaning of faith. Much good might be done by asking pupils to write their own account of the event and then try and illustrate it from a modern standpoint. Teachers could then go on to talk about more abstract expressions of religious ideas. They could also discuss what Christians mean by 'the presence of Jesus'. A project for a display could be developed which showed a number of different ways that people over the centuries have written about and depicted the resurrection, the ascension and the continuing presence of Jesus in people's lives.

The Last Judgement

Other images which can cause confusion, but also provide a challenge, are those known under the title of *The Last Judgement*. The most famous of these is the great painting by Michelangelo for the altar wall of the Sistine Chapel in the Vatican, Rome, painted in 1534–6. This is often found in textbooks and, while a marvellous work of art, is a complex and difficult image, the true interpretation of which is still a matter of argument among scholars. In its basic iconography, however, it is within the long tradition of such images which show Jesus in heaven, sometimes with God depicted as well, blessing the saved and condemning the damned. The souls are usually shown as naked bodies, either rising to heaven or descending to a fiery hell, often complete with horrendous devil forms. Any teacher will, at once, see that these images could be the source of many a nightmare, and indeed that was their purpose. They come from the period before the Reformation and are closely tied into the Roman Catholic doctrines surrounding the judgement of God and the role of the Church in ensuring that damnation was prevented – or at least mitigated. These images can seem strange to a modern child because many people now do not acknowledge this role of the Church, and the fear of hell is less powerful.

With Key Stage 2 and 3 pupils, this theology is probably rather beyond their general capacity. However, if these images are introduced from a *historical* perspective and set within their context, then when pupils encounter them in books and galleries, they can begin to understand why they depict the gruesome scenes in the way they do. An important part of work at this stage, could be discussing what is meant by such words as 'heaven' and 'hell'. In practical terms it could be linked to a discussion of the healing ministry of Jesus and the way in which he always forgave people their sins when they turned to him.

Eucharistic images, including *The Last Supper*

There are also many images which depict interpretations of *eucharistic* theology. Again, most of these come from within Roman Catholic doctrine and need to be seen within the context of the Roman Catholic doctrine of transubstantiation. This is clearly a topic which Key Stage 2 would find too difficult and only the brightest of Key Stage 3 children could tackle easily. These images include such paintings as the famous *Disputà* by Raphael in the Vatican and *The Blood of the Redeemer* by Bellini, which is in the National Gallery in London. Both these images tend to turn up in textbooks.

The best approach to these images at Key Stage 2 would be to explain the symbolism as simply as possible and then to use the discussion as a moment to consider the importance of the Communion or Eucharist in the practice of the Christian Church. Teachers might find it helpful to consult one or more of the books recommended for confirmation candidates, which will touch on these issues. With Key Stage 3, the same approach could be used and, depending on the ability of the pupils, then taken on to a more complex discussion of what Christians believe when they attend a Communion service. Obviously, the spread of belief in this area is wide, ranging from the Orthodox, through the Roman Catholic and Anglo-Catholic, to the Protestant view of the event simply as a remembrance of the Last Supper.

Although *Last Supper* images are probably best introduced in the narrative section, they do, of course, often contain symbolic references to these issues, and it could be helpful to pupils to use a *Last Supper* alongside the purely Eucharistic images, to broaden the discussion and bring it closer to pupils' own experiencc.

THE VIRGIN MARY

Another group of images, linked closely to doctrine, are those depicting the Virgin Mary. Some of these images are, obviously, tied into Roman Catholic doctrine and may not be acceptable to either Protestant groups or members of the Orthodox Church. In the main, the images of the Virgin Mary which are to be found in galleries are those which come from the Roman Catholic tradition. This covers the doctrines of the immaculate conception, the assumption and the coronation of the Virgin, and are contained within paintings or cycles of paintings which deal with *The Life of the Virgin*. Such cycles may also show incidents from the lives of Mary's parents, based on apocryphal (non-gospel) stories about them. Other scenes may depict her own life, including her birth, presentation in the Temple, her life as mother of Christ, and her death and assumption.

A good deal of this material is legendary, and teachers need to know what is based on gospel material and what on legend. However, despite this, within the Roman Catholic faith, these images are perfectly valid because they are now supported by the authority and tradition of the Church. These images will, therefore, have to be treated with sensitivity when the class contains children from different Christian groups and from the Muslim faith. It must be remembered that the Koran gives the Virgin Mary a special place. However, the Muslim pupils will not wish this to be supported by images.

c) The cultural context

It is in this area that the RE teacher can make extensive links across the curriculum to give the work a deeper relevance and meaning. It is also the point at which the use of painting and sculpture can be broadened out from that on strictly religious topics to the great range of art which covers almost every aspect of human life. Religious ideas, from all cultures, reflect the way in which men and women attempt to make sense of their lives. Secular art can address these issues, or point to them, in a rich and challenging way.

One current misconception is that there was no secular art before a certain date. This is simply not true. Artists have always depicted a wide variety of subjects, even within the early medieval world in Western Europe dominated by Christianity. The only reason that the walls of art galleries dealing with this period seem to be dominated by religious images is that religious paintings tend to survive better than secular ones. The reason for this is largely practical. Much secular painting was originally done in fresco on the walls of houses or in tempera or oil on painted furniture. As we all know, people like changing their decorations and their furniture, and so many of these images have now perished and, where discovered beneath later layers, are often in bad condition. However, enough has survived to give us an idea of what such images were like. This means that pupils could, when studying the religious art from a certain period make the connection with the secular art and then look at some of the issues which are raised by the images.

That said, it is, of course, true that since the Reformation secular art has developed extensively because there were many people who did not want religious images but still wanted paintings and sculptures for their homes and public spaces. Since the age of the Enlightenment during the eighteenth century, artists have worked with increasing freedom in all fields and addressed all subjects. Today, there are almost no restrictions on what an artist may depict and artists are often at the forefront of the debate on social issues. This means that, with a little courage, the RE teacher can take a variety of modern and traditional images and use them to help pupils consider some of the issues which are contained in the SCAA/QCA syllabus.

In Model 2, Questions and Teachings, the syllabus has the following Key Ideas and questions arising from human experience for Key Stage 2 Christianity:

- How do we know what someone is like, and how do people show us what they are like?
- Encountering mystery; making sense of the unknown.
- Discerning a purpose in life, and learning from other people's lives.
- Being powerless and vulnerable.
- Sharing other people's experience in order to help them.
- People matter.
- Self-sacrifice for others.
- Release from the past – starting with a clean slate.
- Working together as a team.
- People have different aptitudes, strengths and weaknesses.
- Sharing, interdependence, leadership, rules, responsibilities, obedience, shared identity and purpose.
- Celebration, affirmation, devotion, valuing, offering, thanksgiving.
- Questioning, developing awareness, openness, inspiration, insight, discovery.
- Why do we believe some things and not others?
- Why or what do we respect/follow/believe? Why?

- How people/things with authority affect our lives.
- Who am I? Being special; awareness of not being perfect and of wrongdoing; failure, needing forgiveness; destiny; purpose in life.
- Leadership, loyalty, shared values, sacrifice, setting an example, putting principles into practice, living for a cause/purpose.

For Key Stage 3 Christianity the equivalent section has the following:

- Paradox and mystery at the heart of attempts to understand the natural world
- The use of symbolic language to grapple with the complex nature of reality
- The nature of truth and evidence
- Belief without physical proof – what 'truths' do we accept on the word of another, and what do we not accept?
- Different aspects of being
- The spiritual nature of humanity
- Learning and facing up to the truth about ourselves
- Ways of coming to terms with what we are
- People who rescue us from despair – being able to start again

- The importance of unity; shared ideals and targets
- The benefits and disadvantages of different perspectives and traditions
- How can we disagree and avoid destructive conflict?

- The possibility of the influence on our lives by outsiders
- The feeling that there is 'something there'

- Richness of human language – different forms of expressing what is dear to us, and difficulties of expressing innermost feelings in words
- The importance of having principles and values by which to live
- People and literature, whose words have a deep meaning for us
- The relationship between authority, rules, guidance and free will

- What should people be like?
- What would be the ideal human being in an ideal world?
- Why are we not perfect, and what is the problem?
- How to live by a set of values on a daily basis
- Questions about purpose and identity in life
- The effects of peer group pressure

In the syllabus these questions are linked into the pattern of work for Christianity. However, it is true to say that every one of these major 'life' questions is addressed in one or more images. Art is about life and artists portray life. Architects create buildings which reflect the way human beings need to live their lives. So, with a little research and care, teachers should be able to find images, past and present, which could be used to help the RE work in this area. Sometimes a group of images combining different periods and different techniques can provide a challenging stimulus to a study of a particular social issue and its relationship to belief and practice.

The question could be asked: 'is this a perversion of the reason for the creation of the art?' Can you take a work of art from one period or one situation and use it within a context for which it was not originally intended? Yes, of course, you can, and that is what people have been doing with almost all art ever since it was created. With the exception of a few religious works of art which are still in the churches for which they were created, most works of art are now far both from the artist's studio and the original place of display. Even buildings put up for one purpose have often been adapted, extended or simply redecorated since the concept of the original architect. However, if work is being done with or about art which is now in a different context, then pupils will be helped in their general understanding of that work if they do have some knowledge of its original context.

To give an example of this, I wrote the following description:

> Westminster Abbey was originally built as an abbey church for a monastic foundation by Edward the Confessor. Since then it has developed into the national church and contains within its walls an enormous variety of works of art of all dates. It houses many of the memorials to famous British people and the tomb of the unknown warrior. More recently it has added a memorial to the civilians who have died as a result of war. It has royal tombs and saintly tombs. It has soaring Gothic arches and Victorian alterations. It has icons in the nave and corners of simple Protestant simplicity. At times it is crowded with tourists with little interest in the religious liturgy and at other times it is filled with the glorious sound of the choir singing Evensong and a quiet congregation listening intently. On yet other occasions it is the setting for great state occasions, sometimes happy and sometimes, such as the funeral of the Princess of Wales, of great sadness. It contains a conglomeration

> of artistic ideas and reflects a huge variety of national interests in its activities. However, it is all held together by the central idea of a building set aside for the worship of God, where His love is the central theme of all the variety.

The schemes of work at the end of the book will give suggestions as to how art and architecture, in all their variety, can be harnessed as ways of inspiring pupils to consider some issues and to see their relevance to their everyday lives.

d) Changing styles and traditions

As can be seen from the outline history of Christian art and the summary of artistic developments in Western art, the patterns in art are constantly changing. There are various aspects of this constant change which may be used by the RE teacher to enlarge the approach to the study of Christian life.

MAKING LINKS

The first of these is the fact that while styles and traditions constantly shift and move on, very often current ideas are rooted in the ideas of the past. Just as much of Damien Hirst's work has its roots in some Renaissance imagery, so other modern artists are working with ideas which, because they reflect the age-old questions about life, are based in problems which earlier artists have addressed. Sometimes these links are with earlier Christian art and sometimes with ideas from other cultures. In the Renaissance, for example, there was an enormous revival of interest in the great stories from classical Greek and Roman culture, and these were reflected in many of the works of art. This was fuelled at the time by the discovery of many older sculptures which had long been lost and forgotten. For pupils to realize that say, a striking image from an advertisement has links with art from an earlier period, and also with ideas from an ancient civilization, is to give them a chance to consider religious ideas from a wider standpoint. If it is true that many children find religious education boring and irrelevant, then the use of art to make the connections betweeen religion and society and their own current concerns may help to relieve that boredom. Even a simple grounding in the development of art will give teachers the knowledge they need to spot these connections and develop work in this way. This, of course, is taking the teacher away from specifically religious art, but, if religion is about the whole of life, then images which do not necessarily portray a defined doctrine can still be used to underline a religious idea.

Inspiration from different cultures

Following on from this, many artists are inspired by the artistic work of other cultures. Throughout the ages there has been a cross-fertilization of ideas from one tradition to another. One well-known example is the influence of Japanese prints on the Impressionists during the nineteenth century. Another is the impact of African masks on Picasso and the great South American sculptures in the British Museum on Henry Moore. In earlier periods, Greek civilization had an enormous effect on the way that the Romans developed their buildings and the styles (known as 'orders') they used for their columns. However, as the Roman Empire expanded all over the Middle East, Roman architects were inspired by some of the much more decorative styles that they found in other countries, and Roman buildings in the Middle East and Africa were often decorated in much more elaborate ways. Recently, Alexander McQueen, working for the Paris couturier Givenchy, designed clothes which gave the appearance of direct inspiration from images from the time of the Tudors, such as can be seen in *The Ambassadors* by Holbein, in the National Gallery in London. This painting received extensive coverage in the press just at the time McQueen would have been designing that collection.

Bearing in mind that we are now living in a plural society, where almost every country has a wide mix of races, this cross-fertilization will, no doubt increase. Traditions from other parts of the world will come close to us as they are visualized, either by artists or through the reports we see on television, in magazines and newspapers and on the Internet. It is already becoming apparent that artistic styles are changing with ever-increasing rapidity as artists seek to reflect this cosmopolitan world. For the RE teacher, careful use of some of this material can help to link the religious ideas of some of these groups to the cultural traditions. If pupils can be helped to see how a beautiful or inspiring artistic idea has been used by an artist to enhance their own culture, then they can begin on the task of learning compassion and understanding for the different peoples of the world and for their different faiths.

The constant Christian image

In among this welter of different artistic expression, however, the Christian images have retained a surprising constancy. No doubt this is due, in part, to the control imposed by the Roman Catholic Church after the Council of Trent in the mid-sixteenth century. However, it is also true that the basic Christian ideas have remained constant throughout the last two thousand years. Scholars and theologians may have argued about differences of interpretation, but no one has suggested that the gospels should be completely rewritten, even if textual analysis has suggested caution with some passages. Modern theologians strive for new interpretations, but still the words of St Paul and the other New Testament writers remain our source of inspiration. This is reflected in the constantly recurring themes in Christian art so that, within the endless change of style and interpretation, there is a solid core which remains the same. This is also true, of course, of images of the Buddha and some Hindu images. Pupils could consider this question of the interplay between change and tradition, by using the development of art to point up the place of religious ideas as the bedrock of societies.

e) Discussion and debate

This book has argued that a grounding in the theory of history of art and the use of art as a tool within religious education can help the teacher to broaden the subject and increase its interest value. From my experience of practical research in the classroom, it is clear that the use of images can trigger lively debate and provoke pupils into considering subjects from a new angle. The art and history curricula should provide pupils at both Key Stages 2 and 3 with the basic knowledge and vocabulary with which to discuss these ideas and to express them clearly.

Beauty in art

In this section we come back to the more abstract questions such as the place of beauty in art and the development of spirituality. Clearly a very beautiful painting can be an inspiration, but it is unlikely that all the pupils in any one class will agree as to exactly what constitutes beauty and whether or not a particular object reaches their own standard. This need not inhibit the teacher from introducing this subject for discussion. Indeed, using a variety of images, the teacher can help pupils to develop an aesthetic sense, not only in relation to the question of beauty from a visual point of view but also from the angle of the relationship of beauty created by human beings set alongside the beauty of God's creation.

The beautiful in action

The potential here can perhaps be summed up by the title of Malcolm Muggeridge's book about Mother Teresa which he called *Something Beautiful for God*. Mother Teresa has come under some criticism for her methods from some quarters, but despite that there is no doubt that she did an enormous amount to relieve suffering and to teach us all how to treat the most unfortunate members of society. Her actions reflected that part of human nature which God created and which can act in a beautiful way. Yet her face, as the world came to know it, was the face of an old woman – not perfect gilded youth. Many artists have addressed this question of the difference between the young and the old face – often in a rather sad and unforgiving way. Using some of these contrasting images teachers could develop a wide-ranging discussion.

One of the facts that cannot be avoided in the study of imagery in relation to religious ideas is the wide variety of different attitudes both to the use of religious images and their content if used. This is a subject which has generated terrible actions in the past, with not only large scale destruction of works of art and buildings, but also the persecution, torture and sometimes execution of individuals. However beautiful some of the works of art may be, the subject cannot be divorced from the violence which it has, at times, provoked. The general theme of this book, however, is that, with careful use, even these problems can be used as a way of opening up certain subjects to pupils to help them come to terms with major social issues.

Reworking old ideas

Another facet of the way art is used by those searching for explanations is the way one generation of artists will work over the images of an earlier generation. Leonardo da Vinci's *Last Supper* is an example of this, being reused by generations of artists who use pop art to question many modern assumptions, including Andy Warhol who used the motif for a set of his multiple images. In the *Sensation* exhibition (held at the Royal Academy, London, in 1997), this basic image again occurred in the photomontage *Wrecked*, by Sam Taylor-Wood. This last image, which depicts a bare-breasted female figure standing in the traditional position of Jesus Christ, is one which might need to be handled with some care with certain pupils. However, it does demonstrate the way some modern artists use such conventional images as the various types for *The Last Supper* to debate social issues.

Provided pupils are given a very simple vocabulary with which to discuss the component parts of an image and some historical context, they can then move with great freedom into debate and discussion. The choice of art and architecture which can be used for this purpose is, of course, enormous, and this is only a brief mention of one or two ideas.

6

Putting it into Practice

Four suggested work schemes, with lesson plans, to show ways in which art can be used to develop RE studies

Introductory notes

1. These notes will help teachers to make the best use of the four suggested work schemes provided in this chapter.

2. The schemes are designed to give a general outline of the way a particular form of art or architecture can be used, followed by a set of lesson plans. These are given over five lessons which can be used in the following ways:

a) as a half-term's course project to introduce pupils gradually to the ideas in the scheme;

b) as an intensive one-week project, if the curriculum planning will allow it;

c) as an individual lesson selected from any part of the scheme to enrich or expand existing curriculum plans.

3. Each scheme contains two or three extra key reading suggestions. If teachers have difficulty in obtaining recommended books, they are advised to contact the nearest Art History department in a college or university. Where specialized books are published by museums or galleries, the institution concerned will

be able to advise on ways of obtaining the necessary texts. The reading list notes contain further advice on obtaining information.

4. This book is being published in conjunction with two poster packs (*Images of Jesus Poster Packs*, see page 86), one of traditional images of Jesus and one of more modern images. These packs are based around the following schemes:

a) Traditional Images: Basic Christian Doctrine;

b) Modern Images: Relationships.

Teachers might find it helpful to study the work schemes in these packs, which will provide other approaches. The schemes in this book, however, can be used without this extra support.

5. All the suggestions in this book and the poster packs are based on academic research which was done for a postgraduate degree at the Institute of Education, University of Warwick.

6. Teachers wanting to explore the subject further, or who would like more help in preparing work for pupils, should contact The National Society's RE Centres in London, 36 Causton Street, London SW1P 4AU; Tel: 0171 932 1191) or York (The College of Ripon York St John, Lord Mayor's Walk, York YO3 7EX; Tel: 01904 616858).

Materials required

These schemes, apart from specialized reading, should not require teachers to purchase any extra equipment not normally used in schools. Most of the suggestions can be developed using the pens, pencils, art materials, science and computer equipment which pupils will be using for the work in many parts of the National Curriculum.

Where teachers would like to start pupils using some old and interesting techniques such as the use of egg tempera paint or print-making techniques, they will find that most public libraries have good modern art methods books which cover most of them. If difficulty is encountered, local museums and galleries will almost certainly be able to supply helpful information. Some techniques, such as etching are, of course, potentially dangerous and teachers are advised not to embark on such techniques in the classroom without the support of the art department and without personal experience of the way these techniques function. Many of the simpler and safer methods of art production will provide younger pupils with a stimulating learning experience, so teachers should not feel concerned that they necessarily have to use the more demanding techniques. For example, poster paint applied to a wooden board covered with damp plaster of paris, will give much the same effect, in the short term, as the building of a wall and the application of plaster for a true fresco effect!

In schools where cross-curricular work is the norm, then it should be possible for teachers to draw on practical experience in a number of departments to help them create a useful project. In those schools where the RE teacher is still isolated, the The National Society's RE Centre staff in London and York will be delighted to make suggestions as to where to obtain the necessary technical support.

Suggestions for work using art within the RE Curriculum

The purpose of the section is to suggest to teachers ways in which the SCAA/QCA syllabus recommendations can be supplemented easily and simply to enhance the main curriculum in Religious Education with some work using art and architecture. Mindful of time pressure on teachers and the small number of hours usually allocated to religious education, most suggestions will be quite short.

Scheme 1: The Monastic Life

Gives ways of gaining an insight into the life of monastic communities, including spiritual life and prayer, through an examination of the design and decoration of monasteries and convents.

SCAA/QCA Syllabus: Key Stage 3: Model 1: Learning experiences related to Attainment Targets 1 & 2

Belief in God

1. Explore the ways in which God is portrayed in art, poetry, music and drama in different traditions.
2. Consider experiences which take people beyond everyday events, and which might be interpreted as examples of the spiritual dimension of life.

INTRODUCTION

In the Art curriculum pupils should be taught the main techniques of painting in the early to mid Renaissance. In the History curriculum they should study the medieval and Tudor periods in Britain. Although very little art which was made in Britain remains from that period, following the iconoclasm of the sixteenth and seventeenth centuries, we know that the methods used were the same as those employed in the rest of Europe; also, that before the Reformation, religious practices were much the same throughout Europe. So, taking an artist from Florence, such as Fra Angelico, it would be possible to use one of his images with children at Key Stage 3, to study the use of art in monastic life in the fifteenth century. Fra Angelico painted frescos on the walls of the Monastery of San Marco in Florence and in the Vatican in Rome. He also painted a number of altarpieces on wooden panels for the monastery and other churches, mainly for the Medici family.

Suggested Lesson Plans

Lesson 1 With support from the art department, it would be possible for pupils to recreate a Renaissance image, either a small altarpiece for use in a home or a larger altarpiece for a church. The National Gallery publishes a number of books and videos which describe the techniques used in these processes (see Suggested additional reading *below*). If pupils are near the National Gallery, London, they could visit the Sainsbury Wing to see a number of medieval images. The most important of these for the history of England is *The Wilton Diptych*

Lesson 2 The pupils can then use the image they have created to make a devotional setting from which to consider what it would have been like to pray in a medieval monastery or convent. They could consider what it would be like to live in a cell decorated with religious images, not all of them entirely happy. They could discuss whether it was easier to keep silence when surrounded by images or whether it is easier in a plain setting.

Lesson 3 If the school is near the ruins of an abbey or convent, they could visit it and try to visualize it with the images in place. They could consider what it was like to be a monk or a nun in medieval England or Wales. Alternatively, if there are any medieval churches or cathedrals nearby which still have remains of medieval or early Renaissance frescos, then they could visit them and study what difference they made to the building.

They can then discuss whether art in these settings helps people to believe in God, or whether it is easier to believe in him in some other place such as the open hills or by the sea. Pupils can consider whether a life of prayer, surrounded by images, helps people to believe.

Lesson 4 Using the information gained in the research for Lessons 1 to 3, pupils could then either construct their own paper model of a medieval Christian building, with painted decoration or, if a computer graphics package is available, they could make a video installation. The art, technical drawing and computer departments should be able to help with this. If these facilities are not available in the school, the nearest college of art would probably be able to give helpful advice.

Lessson 5 Drawing on all the information pupils have researched for the earlier lessons, they could then plan an assembly to show the whole school what part painted decoration had to play in medieval Christian buildings. They could also put together a short service, such as Compline, with appropriate music and then, with the whole school joining in, make the subject come alive.

Suggested additional reading

J. Bomford et al. (eds), *Italian Painting before 1400*, Art in the Making series, The National Gallery Publications, 1990.

D. Gordon, *The Wilton Diptych*, Making & Meaning series, National Gallery Publications, 1993.

T. McAleavy, *Life in a Medieval Abbey*, English Heritage Gatekeeper Series, 1998.

N. MacGregor, *Making Masterpieces*, BBC Education in association with National Gallery Publications, 1997 (also available as a video).

Scheme Two: Symbols and Religion

Discusses the use of symbols in art and suggests ways of taking important paintings and using their content to start an examination of the religious period under discussion and its relationship to the politics and history of religion.

SCAA/QCA Syllabus Key Stage 2: Model 1: Learning experiences related to Attainment Target 1

The Church

1. Consider the application of Christian values to specific circumstances, particularly in relation to personal, social and global issues.
2. Talk to Christians about the importance of the Church in their lives.
3. Make a display of objects and symbols associated with Christian worship, and state their use and significance.
4. Find out how two different denominations celebrate the Eucharist
5. Listen to stories associated with important festivals, e.g. Pentecost and the giving of the Holy Spirit.

INTRODUCTION

In the History curriculum for Key Stage 2, Study Unit 2: Life in Tudor Times, pupils should receive a grounding in the history, both social and political, of the period of the Reformation/Renaissance. This means that teachers can select from a wide range of paintings and sculpture from this period to follow through the suggested lesson plans. The National Gallery and the Victoria and Albert Museum, London, have a large number of such objects which can be used. Provincial museums, galleries and large country houses also contain many such paintings and sculptures. Before embarking on this scheme, teachers would be well advised to find out what is available locally, so that pupils can supplement the classroom work with appropriate visits where possible. Education departments of most institutions will be pleased to give support and advice. This scheme can be adapted to earlier or later periods: for example, the Pre-Raphaelites included much symbolism in their paintings. The scheme can also be used either with secular objects or religious ones.

Suggested Lessson Plans

Lesson 1 Having chosen one or two paintings or sculptures from those easily available, teachers can help pupils to study the objects and to make a list of all the people, artefacts, colours and other details. With the aid of reference books, the pupils can then list the meanings of all these details/symbols and examine what the painting or sculpture might mean. Some paintings are quite easy to understand, others much more difficult. An example of an easy one would be Bellini's *Madonna of the Meadow*. A difficult one is Holbein's *Ambassadors*. Both these paintings are in the National Gallery in London.

Lesson 2 Pupils could study some of the different symbols used in Christian art. These could include the dove which represents the Holy Spirit, haloes round the heads of figures to denote holiness and other more unusual ones. They could then make a reference book, listing all the symbols they have discovered and illustrate them with simple line drawings. Where possible pupils could visit the nearest Church and discover what symbols are used there in the furnishings, windows, on the walls and in other places.

Lesson 3 Pupils could then design and make their own religious painting (or a secular painting if they prefer), using some of the symbols they have studied. This painting could include some reference to modern social and political ideas. For example they could use modern 'icons' like the symbols used in road traffic directions or in popular television programmes. They could then discuss whether these modern symbols can represent Christian ideas like the older ones.

Lesson 4 Using the appropriate prayer books pupils can then study the different forms of Eucharist/Holy Communion and then link these services to the descriptions of the Last Supper in the Gospels. With the help of the work on symbols, they can then discuss how different paintings have represented the Eucharist. The Poster Pack *Images of Jesus: Traditional Images*, gives one example of this type of painting: *The Last Supper* by Giampietrino, which is a contemporary copy of the famous painting by Leonardo da Vinci. The Poster Pack gives further ideas for work on this theme.

Lesson 5 Drawing on the work in Lessons 1 to 4, pupils can then prepare an assembly, to show how symbols have been used to tell the Christian story and make the link with Christian life today. They could prepare an 'altar frontal' in paper, with drawings and paintings on it depicting different symbols which could be used for a school Eucharist. They could also make an 'altarpiece' to hang behind the altar for the service and banners to go round the school hall or chapel. Depending on the skills of the pupils, teachers could expand on these ideas: for example, they could make a papier mâché patten and chalice and decorate it with appropriate symbols.

Suggested additional reading

S. Foister et al. (eds), *Holbein's Ambassadors*, Making & Meaning series, National Gallery Publications, 1997.

M. Hinton et al., *Sculpture at the V & A, A Handbook for Teachers*, Victoria & Albert Museum, 1996.

M. Hinton et al., *The Renaissance at the V & A, A Handbook for Teachers*, Victoria & Albert Museum, 1997.

M. Hirst et al. (eds), *The Young Michelangelo*, Making & Meaning series, National Gallery Publications, 1994.

Scheme Three: Sculpture and the Church

Taking one cathedral as an example, this scheme shows the way sculpture has been and still is being used within church buildings as a focus for worship and prayer.

SCAA/QCA Syllabus Key Stage 2: Model 1: Knowledge and Understanding

Prayer

1. The use of stillness and silence in worship.
2. Some well-loved prayers and their meanings.
3. Reasons why people pray.
4. The meaning of prayer.

Introduction

In the Art curriculum pupils should be taught about sculpture and architecture in the context of developing 'their appreciation of the richness of our cultural heritage'. Building on this work teachers should, with the support of the art department where possible, be able to introduce pupils to the basic development of church architecture and the place within it of sculpture. The History curriculum should have given an outline of the history of iconoclasm during the Tudor period so that teachers will be able to explain why many churches now have no sculpture and why some cathedrals and churches now have very modern works in a much older setting. Pupils can use this knowledge to explore the history of the decoration of Christian buildings with statues, carved stone and wood. They can then relate these objects to the various devotional practices of the mainstream churches. Teachers can select a significant church or cathedral from those in their locality. Most cathedrals have bookshops with a good selection of historical and art historical material about the local area. English Heritage, the

National Trust and local museums and galleries can often also supply helpful information.

Suggested Lesson Plans

Lesson 1 Having chosen the church or cathedral for study, pupils can visit the building or read the appropriate literature. They can study the plan of the building, learn about the dates the different parts were erected and note all the places where sculpture used to stand or was part of the fabric of, say, a rood screen or roof. They can note where it is now missing and where it has been replaced.

Lesson 2 Pupils can research and study older forms of worship and prayers which were associated with particular Christian communities and see where these link to particular programmes of sculpture. For example, often a church dedicated to a particular saint will have a statue of that saint and will celebrate the saint's special day (sometimes known as the patronal festival). If the school is close to such a church or associated with it, then pupils could study that saint in particular.

Lesson 3 Pupils could make a small book of prayers, either on a particular topic, or which relate to a particular saint. They could then illustrate the book, either with their own drawings or with postcards etc. from one of the nearby ecclesiastical buildings. Pupils could also write their own prayers for special purposes and consider whether it is better just to have written and spoken prayers or whether a statue or painting makes it easier to understand and to pray.

Lesson 4 Pupils could study those Christian communities, such as the Orthodox Church where the use of icons is still a very important part of the liturgy. They could research the place of icons both in the Orthodox Churches and in the way they are now being used in many other Christian communities. Orthodox icons are always painted after prayer and proper preparation by the artist so pupils could consider whether it helps to make a truly holy object if you are quiet and prayerful when doing so.

Lesson 5 Pupils could prepare an assembly, using some of the prayers they have researched or written, and show how different Christian communities use statues, icons, paintings and other artefacts to help them experience the love of God. They could create a small 'chapel' showing how one saint, or perhaps the Virgin Mary, will be represented and how prayers might be said in that setting.

Suggested additional reading

C. Avery, *Florentine Renaissance Sculpture*, John Murray, 1970.

G. Duchet-Suchaux et al., *The Bible and the Saints,* Flammarion, Paris, 1994.

S. Jenkins, *Windows into Heaven, The icons and spirituality of Russia*, Lion Publishing, 1998.

R. Marsh, *Black Angels, The art and spirituality of Ethiopia*, Lion Publishing, 1998.

E. G. Tasker, *Encyclopedia of Medieval Church Art*, Batsford, 1993.

Note: there are numerous books which give histories of the saints, with illustrations, which can be used as a resource for this scheme.

Scheme Four: Illustrations and Story Telling

Using one well-known old manuscript and one modern book, this scheme show show book illustrations have been used to tell the gospel story.

SCAA/QCA Syllabus Key Stage 3: Model 1: Knowledge and Understanding

The Gospels

1. Passages of the gospels which act as 'windows' into the early Church's understanding of Jesus' identity:
2. Selected passages about Jesus, including his birth, baptism, temptation, transfiguration, relationships with people, suffering, death, resurrection and ascension.
3. The idea of the Gospels as good news.
4. The different emphases of the Gospel writers.
5. How the written word portrayed Jesus as the fulfilment of Old Testament messianic prophecies.
6. The relationship between events in the life of Jesus and major Christian festivals.

Introduction

There are many outstanding examples of old manuscripts in British collections, such as the Lindisfarne Gospels or the Book of Kells. Some of these are in mainstream collections such as that of the British Library in London. Others are still kept in cathedral libraries, local museums or public record offices. Teachers are advised to do some preliminary reading in order to decide what type of manuscript they wish the pupils to study. They can then locate the nearest available one in their own locality and obtain supporting literature and, if possible, arrange for pupils to visit the place where it is kept and have a look at it. If, however, they decide to study one of the more important books such as the Lindisfarne Gospels, then there are plenty of reference books which cover them and local libraries should be able to obtain them.

In order to make an effective contrast, teachers can then select one or more modern illustrated books, Bibles or prayer books. These could be books in the school library, selected from the pupils' own books at home or borrowed from the shelves of the local library. There are, of course, an enormous number of illustrated books since about the fifth century AD and teachers are advised to make a careful selection of the periods to be considered. One good time would be the Victorian period when improvements in printing techniques and the introduction of colour plates prompted a quick advance in the variety of illustrations available. The art department should have given pupils a basic grounding in the art of hand illumination and the main printing techniques.

Suggested Lesson Plans

Lesson 1

Using the old manuscript selected, pupils could study its history, how it was made and the style and quality of the illuminations (illustrations). They could research the way many of these manuscripts were produced by monks and nuns and how some of them were also painted by very important artists for rich patrons – such as the *Très Riches Heures* (Very Rich book of Hours) made for the Duc de Berry at the beginning of the Renaissance. Pupils could compare the work done in monasteries and convents with these more luxurious productions which often contained quite secular images even though they were books of prayers and gospel readings.

Lesson 2

Using the modern book, pupils could again study who wrote and illustrated it, how it was printed and how the illustrations were made. They could consider whether the illustrations were appropriate for the subject of the book and discuss whether the story or text would have been easier or less easy to follow if there were no illustrations. Pupils could make a list of say six modern books and prepare a project showing all the details of their production.

Lesson 3

Using the techniques now often taught, pupils could make their own books. They can do this either by repeat folding one sheet of paper, or by cutting several sheets to size and then stitching or stapling them together. They could then write out a chapter from one of the gospels or the Acts of the Apostles or some prayers. Pupils could then create illustrations for their books, either by drawing and painting or by using a simple printing technique. Pupils can then compare their different books and discuss how effective the illustrations are in expressing the ideas in the written text.

Lesson 4

Choosing one of the SCAA/QCA suggested topics on the gospels, the teacher can then ask pupils to say how they would illustrate a book to bring out the importance of the gospel message. Pupils could set up a debate between those who think that the Word should be just that – spoken or written – and those who think the Word is much easier to understand if there are pictures to help.

Lesson 5

Pupils can then plan an assembly, drawing on the work in Lessons 1 to 4, which shows how we have come to accept that almost all books are illustrated. Pupils could make a very large book, like a medieval choir book, from which they could read a short service of prayer and praise, to show how early manuscripts were used in churches and chapels. Alternatively, they could make a small book, like a book of hours and use that in a more devotional setting.

Suggested extra reading

P. Goldman, *Victorian Illustrated Books 1850–1870*, British Museum Press, 1994.

P. Goldman, *Victorian Illustration*, Scolar Press, 1996.

A. Griffiths, *Prints and Printmaking*, British Museum Publications, 1980.

C. de Hamel, *A History of Illuminated Manuscripts*, Phaidon Press, 1986.

Local cathedral or public libraries will be able to advise on the best literature about manuscripts in the area.

Appendix
Reading into the Subject

Guidance on reading Art History for the RE teacher, including a short reading list

The History of Art courses in most colleges and universities cover a wide range of art and architecture. If teachers want to take their studies further, or need advice on reading, they are advised to contact their nearest college or university for support. Advice is also available from the Association of Art Historians who can advise on all matters pertaining to the study of History of Art: Association of Art Historians, Cow Cross Street, Clerkenwell, London, EC1M 6BP (tel: 0171 490 3211).

Most major museums and galleries now have an education department. Their staff can provide support and advice. The reading list below is not comprehensive, but is designed to give teachers a starting point for their work. The bibliographies in individual books will lead on to more detailed reading.

The Pelican History of Art series is a good starting point for gaining useful background about various periods. The Victoria and Albert Museum and the National Gallery also provide a range of resources specifically for the teacher.

General Books

E. H. Gombrich, *The Story of Art*, Phaidon Press, 1996 (1st edn 1950).

F. Hartt, *History of Italian Renaissance Art*, Thames & Hudson, 4th edn, 1994.

M. Henig, (ed.) *A Handbook of Roman Art*, Phaidon Press, 1983.

H. W. Janson, *History of Art*, Thames & Hudson, 5th edn, 1995.

J. Lowden, *Early Christian and Byzantine Art*, Phaidon Press, 1997.

N. Pevsner, *An Outline of European Architecture*, Penguin Books, 1985 (1st edn 1943).

G. M. A. Richter, *A Handbook of Greek Art*, Phaidon Press, 9th edn, 1987.

N. Stangos (ed.) *Concepts of Modern Art*, Thames & Hudson, 1981.

L. White, *Art and Architecture in Italy*, 1250–1400, Penguin Books, 1987.

REFERENCE BOOKS

I. Chilvers and H. Osborne (eds) *The Oxford Dictionary of Art*, Oxford University Press, 1997.

F. L . Cross (ed.) *The Oxford Dictionary of the Christian Church*, Oxford University Press, 1957; 2nd edn, 1974.

J. Hall, *Dictionary of Subjects and Symbols in Art*, John Murray, 1987.

P. and L. Murray, *The Oxford Companion to Christian Art & Architecture*, Oxford University Press, 1996.

J. Speake, *Dent Dictionary of Symbols in Christian Art*, J. M. Dent, 1994.

ART HISTORY THEORY

J. Berger, *Ways of Seeing*, BBC and Penguin Books, 1972.

A. Derbes, *Picturing the Passion in the Late Medieval Italy*, Cambridge University Press, 1996.

Griffiths, *Prints and Printmaking*, Trustees of the British Museum, 1980.

E. Welch, *Art & Society in Italy*, 1350–1500, Oxford History of Art, 1997.

Inspired by *Using Art in RE: Using RE in Art?*

*Use **Images of Jesus Poster Packs** to illustrate your passion for art.*

Both packs – traditional and modern – include five beautiful A2 full-colour laminated posters. Their accompanying booklets provide background notes to the artists and their style, as well as practical activities for use with children or young people.

The **traditional** pack includes works by well known artists ● *Madonna and Child with Angels*, Gentile da Fabriano ● *The Baptism of Jesus*, Piero della Francesca ● *The Last Supper*, Attributed to Giampietrino ● *Scenes from the Passion*, The Master of Delft ● *The Miraculous Draught of Fishes*, Raphael

ISBN 0 7151 4898 2 **Price £19.95**

The **modern** pack focuses on Jesus' encounters with people throughout his life on earth. The images chosen are selected to show a wide multi-cultural diversity and include images by Sri Lankan, African and Asian artists.

● *Nativity Scene 1990*, Beryl Cook ● *Jesus and the Children* (Jésus et les Enfants), Madame Benedit de l'Eroncière ● *Jesus at Bethany*, Winitha Fernando ● *The Crucifixion*, John Reilly ● *The Road to Emmaus*, He Qi

ISBN 0 7151 4917 2 **Price £19.95**

No classroom deserves to be without them.

Place an order with your local bookstore or call 0171 898 1301/1302 to order direct. Website: www.chpublishing.co.uk